CW01313332

Your Identity in Christ Jesus

Your glorious adoption and your royal identity

Chris Eke

First published by Createspace (USA) an Amazon company in 2017

Copyright © Christopher Eke 2017

The right of Christopher Eke to be identified as the Author of the Work has been asserted by him in accordance with the Copyright, Designs and Patents Act 1988.

All rights reserved. No part of this publication may be reproduced, stored in a retrieval system, or transmitted, in any form or by any means without the prior written permission of the publisher, nor be otherwise circulated in any form of binding or cover other than that in which it is published and without a similar condition being imposed on the subsequent purchaser.

ISBN 978 1501053986

All Bible quotes are taken from the English Standard Version unless stated otherwise.

Contents

Introduction 9

FROM THE STREETS TO THE PALACE: YOU ARE ADOPTED 14

    Adoption 15

    Your Royal Adoption 18

    It means: Family relationship 20

    It means: Father is in control 21

    It means: We have an inheritance 23

    It means: Restoration of self-worth 25

    It means: Victory over the kingdom of darkness 27

LIVING IN YOUR NEW IDENTITY 34

    Story of Celestine 34

    Identity Crisis 36

    Relating to Celestine's story 37

YOUR IDENTITY AND KINGDOM MINISTRY 46

    Our identity as children of God 48

    Our identity as servants and stewards of God 50

YOUR IDENTITY AND THE QUESTION OF YOUR SALVATION ... 68

    Is it once saved, always saved OR am I being saved, for which I have a part to play in its completion? Which one is it?! 69

    Once saved always saved 71

    Predestination and Election: A stronger case for once saved always saved 77

The case for salvation by grace through faith as evident in a transformed heart 82

THE ROYAL DISCIPLINE 100

The Royal Standard 100

Discipline in outward appearance 103

Discipline in Grace 111

The Loving but firm discipline of the Lord 115

HEAVENLY SONS, EARTHLY EXPERIENCES 124

Seasons of life 124

More knowledge and understanding of one's new identity 129

Improved prayer life and fellowship with God 130

More daring faith 132

Maturing as a believer 141

MATURITY IN YOUR NEW IDENTITY 152

Being a part of a church 153

Reading and studying the Word of God 154

Listening to sermons and reading other Christian books 158

Obeying and practicing biblical principles and teachings.... 161

Introduction

The word identity is broad in its meaning, incorporating words like uniqueness, character, personality, individuality, among others. Generally, the word points to a person or a thing's unique attributes or characteristics be it physical, relational or personality that differentiates it from others. The question of identity is central in defining our way of life and the choices we make. Identify yourself with anything and it could shape your thinking and the course of your life. Such is the power of understanding your identity.

As Christians, we believe our identity finds its source from the essence of God, giving us a distinct life that is coded in our DNA and revealed in our features and personality. Our identity is not only personal but it is also global, interlinking us to many other groups while demonstrating variations and similarities that points back to us. What I mean is: I, Chris Eke, was born in Ghana to a Nigerian dad and a Ghanaian mum. For that reason, I have a national identity of Ghana and Nigeria. This is however an identity I share with approximately twenty million Ghanaians and over one hundred and seventy million Nigerians although it is still my identity. I was born to the Eke family, providing me with an identity reflective in my surname, but then, I also have family members who share in this same identity. In sports, I love football and I support Arsenal FC. This is the club that my friends will identify me with, but on the wider scale I belong to a group of millions of Arsenal FC fans worldwide. My earthly identity therefore, while unique in its sense is interlinked to the world around me. This identity separates and distinguishes me from all creation, and yet it also associates and connects me with others.

Each and every one of us would recognise that we yearn for security and significance in this world, yet we must also recognise that God has created within us a spiritual dimension and an eternal existence. As Christians, our new identity in Christ is not of this world but of Heaven

(Philippians 3:20). Our yearning to belong is therefore not for the things of this world but for the things of Heaven. When a person takes on this new identity, the struggle is often between the heavenly yearnings of the new-self and the earthly desire for the world. This opposing feeling is often a constant battle that if not given careful attention, could leave one occupied by the things of this world and blinded to the reality of their spiritual dimension which is their true identity in Christ.

Our new identity is however attained by faith and lived by faith, hence we must be in tune with the things of faith in order to experience this reality. The book of Hebrews states that; *"Now faith is the assurance of things hoped for, the conviction of things not seen"* (Hebrews 11:1). The challenge is therefore between having to live according to the things you see and the truth of the things not seen.

In Christ, the Bible explains we have been adopted as sons (Galatians 4:4-6), making us children of God (1 John 3:2). This is our new identity, and by our understanding of this truth we can partake of the divine nature. Knowing your identity empowers you to live a Spirit-filled life, equipping you to overcome the domain of darkness as well as ministering in the gifts of the Holy Spirit. This revelation brings you to a place of knowing that Jesus did not only die for us to be forgiven sinners, but even more, His death purchased our adoption and gave us the right to be children of God.

The aim of this book is to enlighten the reader to these biblical truths that leads to brokenness, humility and awe of God's great love for us in Christ. The book will endeavour to act as a mirror that reflects our true identity based on scriptural truth and not on fallible words of human knowledge. May the Lord open your heart to receive His words and empower you to walk in this newness of life.

Yours in Christ,
Chris Eke

From The Streets To The Palace: You Are Adopted

FROM THE STREETS TO THE PALACE: YOU ARE ADOPTED

In Paul's letters to the churches, the Apostle often used illustrative words to describe or explain the mystery of the Gospel that is now revealed to us. He did this to enlighten us of the reality of our true identity in Christ. In 2 Corinthians 5:17, the Apostle said, *"Therefore, if anyone is in Christ, he is a new creation. The old has passed away; behold, the new has come"*.

This passage depicts an image of death and birth. It speaks of something old dying off and something new being born or created that never existed before. This idea can be related to Jesus' teaching when he said to Nicodemus, *"Truly, truly, I say to you, unless one is born again he cannot see the kingdom of God"* (John 3:3). This is said to be the view of a spiritual new birth, similar to a child being born into a family. Before birth, the child never existed; but after conception and birth that child now exists and is part of a family. In this view, we can say before we came to faith we never existed in God's family, but in Christ, we have been born into God's family. Dr Neil Anderson sheds some light on this view in his book, Victory Over The Darkness. In it he said, *"A Christian, in terms of his or her deepest identity, is a saint, a spiritually born child of God, a divine masterpiece, a child of light, a citizen of heaven. Being born again transformed you into someone who didn't exist before"*[1]. This is the view of being born again.

The second view is the idea of adoption, which speaks of us being adopted into God's family. In this view, before we came to faith we did not belong to God's family. We were orphans alienated from God, but through faith in Christ, we have been saved and adopted by God.

---

[1] Anderson, N,T. 2002. *Victory Over The Darkness*. California. Regal Books, a division of GL Publications

Ultimately, both views speak of a common truth which is to say that we have a new identity now; be it through adoption or birth, we are now children of God. This book will however focus on the view of adoption, as it will help us understand some of the common challenges we may face on our journey as Christians.

Adoption

In his letter to the church of Ephesus, the Apostle said; *"he* [God] *predestined us for **adoption as sons** through Jesus Christ, according to the purpose of his will"* (Ephesians 1:5). Again, Paul referred to the view of adoption as he exhorted the church of Galatia by saying; *"But when the fullness of time had come, God sent forth his Son, born of woman, born under the law, to redeem those who were under the law, so that we might receive **adoption as sons**. And because you are sons, God has sent the Spirit of his Son into our hearts, crying, "Abba! Father!"* (Galatians 4:4-6).

To clearly understand this truth, one must carefully consider what **adoption** means. Adoption carries the notion of acceptance, welcoming, approval etc., but more so, adoption as relating to a child is often pictured as a process whereby a child is accepted into a family not as a visitor or a guest, but as a member of that family. The formal process of adoption goes much deeper than that, since the adoptive parents are bound by law to assume all parental responsibility in raising and caring for that child. Additionally, in most cases, all ties to the birth parents are severed by law and transferred to the new parents.

In Paul's day, the significance of adoption carried a greater weight especially in the Roman Empire. In his commentary on the book of Romans, William Barclay detailed the process and the significance of the adoption that Paul uses to describe the relationship between the believer and God. In his commentary he said;

"Roman adoption was always rendered more serious and more difficult by the Roman **patria potestas**. The **patria potestas** was the father's power over his family; that power was absolute; it was actually the power of absolute disposal and control, and in the early days it was actually the power of life and death. In regard to his father a Roman son never came of age. No matter how old he was, he was still under the **patria potestas**, in the absolute possession, and under the absolute control, of his father. Obviously this made adoption into another family a very difficult and a very serious step. In adoption a person had to pass from one **patria potestas** to another. He had to pass out of the possession and control of one father into the equally absolute possession and control of another. There were two steps. The first was known as **mancipatia**, and it was carried out by a symbolic sale, in which copper and scales were symbolically used. Three times the symbolism of sale was carried out. Twice the father symbolically sold his son, and twice he bought him back; and the third time he did not buy him back, and thus the **patria potestas** was held to be broken. After the sale there followed a ceremony called **vindicatio**. The adopting father went to the praetor, one of the Roman magistrates, and presented a legal case for the transference of the person to be adopted into his **patria potestas**. When all this was completed then the adoption was complete. Clearly this was a serious and an impressive step.

But it is the consequences of adoption which are most significant for the picture that is in Paul's mind. There were four main consequences. (i) The adopted person lost all rights in his old family, and gained all the rights of a fully legitimate son in his new family. In the most literal sense, and in the most binding legal way, he got a new father. (ii) It followed that he became heir to his new father's estate. Even if other sons were afterwards born, who were real blood relations, it did not affect his rights. He was inalienably co-heir with them. (iii) In law, the old life of the adopted person was completely wiped out. For instance, legally all debts were cancelled; they were wiped out as if they had never been. The adopted person was regarded as a new person entering into a new life with which the past had nothing to do. (iv) In the eyes of the law the adopted person was literally and absolutely the son of his new father"[2].

In this context, we can perceive the radical transformation the Apostle speaks of, when he says we are now adopted children of God. It is obvious that in Christ we are not the same anymore, something significant has taken place. Similar to the Roman adoption, our old life is completely erased. Meaning, all our debts of sin and the legal requirement to bring us into judgement is averted through this adoption. Furthermore, what sort of stigma were you living under before you came to faith? Consider that life done away with! If you were spiritually impoverished, bound by the forces of darkness with no hope or clear reason for existence; this is now changed by God's grace through adoption. In this adoption, we now have hope for today and for the future. To this end, Apostle Paul said, *"The Spirit himself bears witness with our spirit that we are children of God, and if children, then heirs—heirs of God and fellow heirs with Christ, ..."* (Romans 8:16-17).

This passage further emphasizes that, not only are you a child of God now, but as the earthly process of adoption guarantees the adopted child the right to inheritance, likewise, you also have an inheritance in the Kingdom of God. Believe it or not, Heaven is a part of your inheritance. You now have a share in Heaven's power and authority through Christ. Because of this wonderful grace, consider yourself a winner not a loser; because you have been adopted to the winning side. Consider yourself a success not a failure, because He who is all able is

---

[2] Barclay, W., 1966. *The Letter to the Romans*. 6th ed. The Saint Andrew Press Edinburgh

ir loving Father, and more so, He has given you of His Spirit and power.

This is a call to renew your mind by the knowledge of this adoption. Draw closer as a child of God and perceive the power He has entrusted to you. Believe in who God says you are in Christ, and walk in this newness of life.

Your Royal Adoption

The magnitude of what was accomplished by Christ' death and resurrection cannot be entirely grasped to the human mind. We can often try and make some sense of it by accepting some key truths of what this death and resurrection means for us. Some of these key truths are; we as believers have been forgiven of our sins, we have been saved from eternal damnation, and that we are loved by God. These are general truths most Christians believe, however when we look at the notion of adoption, it brings the perception of this renewed relationship with God through Christ even closer to our earthly reality.

Although adoption has existed for thousands of years, the twenty-first century has seen a rise in interracial adoption where couples from one ethnic background happily adopt children belonging to another. This type of adoption has been made popular by celebrities such as Angelina Jolie and Brad Pitt, who adopted underprivileged children from different continents of the world. It is often believed that the wealth and fame of these celebrities will help offer a better life for the adopted children, as opposed to the opportunities they may have if they were still orphans. While we do not know what the future holds for any child, we acknowledge the fact that children raised up in a loving and secured home free from poverty and extreme suffering, will have a better chance of doing well in society. Whereas this notion isn't true for all cases, it still holds a general truth for majority, considering the educational opportunities wealth and riches can buy. There is therefore the general expectation for children from wealthy families to achieve a greater social status that reflects the identity of that family.

This example of a celebrity adopting an orphan from a lowly background can give us some glimpse into our adoption as sons of God in Christ Jesus. An even better example to clearly depict this form of adoption can be compared to the Royal Family of England adopting a child into their family.

Picture the Queen of England on a visit to Somalia, a country torn apart by over two decades of civil war. Imagine that during the Queen's visit, she spotted an orphan on the streets whose parents were tragically killed during the war. Being deeply moved with compassion, she took unprecedented steps to adopt that child as hers. Imagine you were that child who was now adopted by the Queen of England. Once the adoption documents are signed, this totally changes everything about you. Your identity is no longer an orphan but a royal child. Your citizenship is no longer Somalian but now British. Where you were once considered less significant, your life and security is now of the upmost regard. The change in your lifestyle and social status from the streets in war torn Somalia to Buckingham Palace of England is enormous, and it will take some time to adjust to. You will have to unlearn a lot of bad habits and therapeutically transform your thinking from that of an orphan to a prince or a princess. This transition could be a struggle and could take years, but the truth is, you are now a royal child by adoption.

If we consider the great privilege of being adopted into an earthly Royal Family, how much more privileged are we to be adopted by God Almighty; the One whose splendour is matchless and beyond any description or human comprehension. Paul the Apostle saw this glory of the Lord and was left speechless (2 Corinthians 12:2-4); as no words or human efforts could suffice to describe the surpassing reality of this glory. This amazing God has now adopted us through Christ as His children. This illustration of a Royal adoption gives us a glimpse into the great privilege of being adopted children of God. But the question is, what does this adoption mean for us?

It means: Family relationship

When you were an orphan on the streets of war torn Somalia, you were on your own; you did not belong to a family. But since you were adopted by the Queen, this has brought you into a relationship with her and the others in the Royal Family. You are no longer on your own anymore, you now have a father, mother, brothers and sisters.

Similarly, being adopted into God's family brings us into a relationship with God where we can confidently call Him our Father and in return be called children. An integral part of any relationship is the love and understanding that binds one to the other. God's love is an unconditional love that brings joy and peace to the redeemed soul. It also gives one the reassurance of security and belonging to the family, while casting away fear of judgement or hostility. Apostle John gives us an insight into this kind of love when he said; *"There is no fear in love, but perfect love casts out fear. For fear has to do with punishment, and whoever fears has not been perfected in love"* (1 John 4:18). On the other hand, this love is patient with us, but it will by no means leave us undisciplined. This discipline is often uncomfortable but God's love will gradually shape us and mould us into the likeness of Christ.

Being adopted into God's family also gives us access to Him. We are no longer alienated from Him, as we have been brought near through the atonement of Christ that cleanses us and grants us that access. We can hence fellowship with our Father through worship and prayer. This access means we do not have to wait for specific days or rely on specific people to enter on our behalf. Christ is our only mediator in whom we have our adoption and identity as sons. Through Him, we have access to our Father as well as His full attention at anytime and anywhere.

This relationship also brings us into intimacy and openness with God. In the security of a family, all pretence or façade is taken down. One is open to others and can be themselves without much concern about what others think of them. Their true character and personality is known by all. Their weaknesses, vulnerability and imperfections are visible for all to see. As adopted children, we have been called to come as we are. There is no need for pretence or concealing our worries, struggles or fears because God sees us as we are. If you are struggling with e.g. alcoholism, pornography, gambling etc., just go to the throne room of grace through prayer and lay it at your Father's feet. There is no need to pretend about it because He already knows. It is however in your transparency and honesty of confession, that He gives you the grace and strength to overcome these struggles. God is not like our earthly parents who as teenagers we could hide our smoking and drinking from. He sees and knows everything about you, yet He is patient and encourages you to draw near to receive mercy and grace to overcome those struggles. If there was ever a person you can be real or open with, it is God.

You are an adopted child of God who is much loved by Him. There is not a moment He is not with you. His love has saved you through Christ and it is this love that has brought you into a relationship with him.

It means: Father is in control

One of the many privileges of being raised in a loving family with a responsible father and mother is the total dependency on their care, protection and provision. Sadly, the reality for many orphan street kids is that, their circumstances leave them independent even though they are ill-prepared for such a life. Our adoption into God's family brings us into a relationship where God is in partnership with us, but more so, in control of our lives. The beauty of this truth means we don't have to face our challenges and troubles alone. We can now depend on our Father to intervene in our affairs, while trusting in His guidance and leadership in our daily lives. This dependency is not one that encourages or tolerates forgoing our responsibility. It is rather the dependency and divine intervention in the areas where one has little or no control over.

Since I came to faith, I have had numerous experiences of God's divine guidance, provision, protection and even discipline. My life is totally dependent on Him, but it took me a while to understand who was truly in control. This is not to say that I do not have a mind of my own. Indeed, I made my daily decisions but as the proverb says, "*Many are the plans in the mind of a man, but it is the purpose of the Lord that will stand*" (Proverbs 19:21).

This is true for all Christians, so just an encouragement not to be overly frustrated with life when it appears all doors leading to your desired goals are closed. In those times, just remember that God is still in control. He opens great doors of opportunities in the right season, but He also shuts doors, even windows that may lead us out on an undesirable path. I can particularly relate to this experience in my season of waiting. It felt like every door I tried to open was locked. Even when it seemed I had broken the door down, what was behind was a brick wall. As frustrating as this season was, it was necessary to build my character, my faith and redirect my focus in discovering my calling to serve the church.

For others who may be struggling financially, do not be surprised when a friend who does not know of your circumstances unexpectedly sends you some money in your desperate need. Your Father knows you need it, hence He has provided for you. This form of divine provision is something I am familiar with. In my experience, it appears that the amount I often receive is just what I needed to see me through. Although I know the Lord can bless us beyond our imagination, I have found that He does not spoil His children. He gives us just enough at a time to teach us how to manage what we have and be good stewards of what has been entrusted to us. As we mature in our understanding and management of these, He entrusts more to us.

As children of God, we are not only meant to be expectant of receiving His provision, but we are also meant to be expectant of hearing from Him. Some of the pivotal moments in my life were times when God spoke and instructed me through dreams. Some dreams came as a warning to steer me away from trouble. Others were to instruct me of the season I was in, giving me a glimpse of where God was leading me. I wish this form of divine updating will happen all the time, but the reality is, God sovereignly speaks through dreams and other means when He chooses.

Ultimately, because God is our Father, the Apostle encourages us to cast all our burdens on Him because He cares for us (1 Peter 5:7). Oh! Such great love and comfort to know that we can find rest amidst the storm because our Father is in control.

It means: We have an inheritance

According to most laws, especially in the Roman view of adoption, the adopted child enjoys the same rights and privileges of a biological child. With regards to inheritance, they are entitled to it where the parents left no will. Similarly, as adopted children of God, Paul the Apostle made a statement about our identity and inheritance in Christ. He said, *"The Spirit himself bears witness with our spirit that we are children of God, and if children, then heirs—heirs of God and fellow heirs with*

Christ, provided we suffer with him in order that we may also be glorified with him" (Romans 8:16-17).

Our adoption has made us sons of God, having the right to inherit or receive that which is of God. This inheritance speaks of our share in the Kingdom of God. It speaks of our share in the New Heaven and the New Earth, the New Jerusalem detailed in Revelation 21:1-27 and Revelation 22:1-5. The Apostle goes further to say, *"In him you also, when you heard the word of truth, the gospel of your salvation, and believed in him, were sealed with the promised Holy Spirit, who is the guarantee of our inheritance until we acquire possession of it, to the praise of his glory"* (Ephesians 1:13-14).

This passage speaks of the assuredness of our inheritance, since we have been sealed with the Holy Spirit as a guarantee (or a down payment) of our inheritance. This simply means, because the Holy Spirit (the third person of the Trinity) has been sent to dwell in us, his presence can only be evident of the reality that we are adopted children of God. The death of a believer or the coming of the Lord will only be our call home to inherit that which is rightfully ours through adoption in Christ. Our adoption has therefore brought us into something far greater than just being a forgiven sinner. We actually have a glorious home prepared for us in Heaven; the beauty of such one cannot comprehend as it is far beyond what we could ever imagine. The idea of having a home in Heaven is not a fairy tale or some irrational fantasy. It is simply what any parent will do for their children; and we are children of the One who created everything seen and unseen who dwells in Heaven. Furthermore, the Lord Jesus said, *"In My Father's house are many mansions; if it were not so, I would have told you. I go to prepare a place for you. And if I go and prepare a place for you, I will come again and receive you to Myself; that where I am, there you may be also"* (John 14:2-3) NKJV.

Ultimately, our inheritance is to be with God and to dwell in His presence. He is the inheritance that satisfies us for eternity. Be encouraged by this truth, and although you may go through struggles in this life, always remember your inheritance that awaits you at the crossing of the finish line.

It means: Restoration of self-worth

If we consider how an adoption from a lowly background into the Royal Family changes everything about a person's identity and self-esteem; this could give us an insight into how our adoption into God's family restores our self-worth. In our analogy, you were an orphan adopted from war-torn Somalia into the Royal Family. Living the life of an orphan street kid could be damaging to one's sense of worth. Having to live life on the streets, often hungry, begging for food, dressed in shabby clothes and most importantly with no family, could create a sense of unworthiness in one's mind. The good news is that, **you were an orphan street kid, but you are now a prince or a princess through adoption**. Although this is true, the psychological effect of living the life of a street kid could take a while before one's true self-worth is realised. The problem is; how could an orphan street kid possibly conceive or even imagine what the esteem of a prince or a princess is like, when in reality all they know is the life of a street kid? It is clear that this process will take a while, however it is by embracing one's new identity that leads to this renewal.

Similarly, as a child of God, you must embrace your new identity and leave behind the things of the past. You shouldn't look down on yourself as though you were a loser or unworthy of God's love and favour. If your past life prior to faith was marked with a lifestyle of sin and unworthiness, in Christ your self-worth is restored. **Example**: If you were a prostitute prior to coming to faith (faith meaning, not only trusting in Christ for salvation but also repenting and walking in the newness of life), you should no longer be identified as such, and hence your self-worth should not be tied to your past. You are now a child of God and a princess of the King.

Realising your identity and self-worth gradually changes your perception and outlook in life. Where you once found your self-worth in money, material possessions, position of power, or even another person, in Christ, you will now find your primary self-worth in the truth of your identity while everything else becomes secondary. What I mean is, the primary self-worth of a king is not rooted in his wealth or possession, even though his wealth or possession may speak of who he is. In truth, his primary self-worth springs from the knowledge of his identity as a king and from this flows respect, authority and the right to command the wealth he has. On the other hand, a thief who has made millions out of robbing and stealing from others will be known as a thief or a criminal regardless of how much they possess. That person may desire the esteem of a noble man but their identity makes them fall short of true nobility.

Realising your self-worth as a child of God puts things into perspective, where your integrity and principles as a Christian is of the upmost value. A child of God cannot be bought at any price at the expense of kingdom values. A child of God understands who they really are and hence will not bend to the standards or trends of the world. You are royalty (not implying lavish living but rather in principle and integrity), hence you live as such.

It means: Victory over the kingdom of darkness

Often in scripture, we see certain passages that depict an image of fierce contention between good and evil. It is from this idea that we are encouraged to put on the whole armour of God in Ephesians 6:10. But the truth over our lives as children of God is that, *"we are more than conquerors through him who loved us"* (Romans 8:37). The Apostle made this bold statement because in actual fact, all power belongs to our God and Jesus Christ our Saviour. There is no contention when God puts his foot down. Over and over again, we see this in scripture from the Old Testament to the New Testament, that all power belongs to God.

In Jesus' ministry, we see how demons obeyed His voice and commands. In Luke 8:26-37, we are told how the demons actually shuddered before Him and pleaded with Him not to cast them out into the abyss. At His command saying, "GO" (Matthew 8:32), the demons departed from the possessed man. In the ministry of the disciples, we also see the same display of power and authority over the domain of darkness. It is undeniably clear that there is no contention when God's Spirit and power is present.

As children of God born again by the Holy Spirit, we now belong to God's Kingdom with great power and authority. We have been adopted from the devil's domain into God's domain, hence the devil has no power or authority over us anymore. A key part of adoption is the transfer of all legal rights and responsibility relating to the child from the biological parents to the adoptive parents. We know that God is sovereign and has never lost any rights over us even when we were lost sinners; but for illustrative purposes using the teaching of adoption, let us assume this was the case.

In this view, we can say being adopted as a child of God transfers all rights from the devil's domain to God's domain. Furthermore, our royal identity as children of God also implies that we can speak with the authority of our Father and the domain of darkness will obey. It is however important to note that we need to be knowledgeable of this authority we have in Christ, since we are faced with a rebellious enemy who will not back down until the day appointed for his judgement. He will still fight against God's children even though he knows he is fighting a losing battle.

One of the devil's trick is to question your identity or make you waver in faith. A good example is found in the Gospel of Mathew, when the devil tried to tempt Jesus during His time of fasting and prayer. It is important to note that the devil had no doubt about Jesus' identity. He knew Jesus was the Son of God and the Second Person of the Trinity, but he still sought to sow seeds of doubt. He started his first two questions by saying, *"If you are the Son of God"*, do this or do that. This is a deceptive way the devil attacks, because he knows that the knowledge of your identity is your victory over him. A prince or a princess who does not know of their royal identity and authority can be disrespected, abused or even mistreated. The devil's first attack is to make you question your identity. The one who does not know his/her identity and authority as a child of God is vulnerable to the devil's tricks and relentless attacks. However, if you know who you are in Christ, you can resist the enemy or use your authority to declare God's truth over your life.

Through my journey of faith, I have come to realise that most of our fiercest battles are fought in our minds. I believe there are different levels the enemy attacks us in this way.

Level 1.

He attacks us by sowing seeds of doubt concerning our faith and identity as Christians. This often happens when a believer is new to the faith or may not have grasped the core message of the Gospel. At this stage, the believer is vulnerable to deceptive teachings of false prophets and teachers, since they are lacking in the fundamental knowledge of truth.

Level 2.

The devil attacks us through various forms of temptations e.g. sex, love of money, drugs etc. He will attack you where he knows you have a weakness. Sometimes the attack is well orchestrated, it's just perfect and well hidden.

He may whisper and say, *'Just relax, you are on holiday alone and no one knows you are a Christian here. Go on! A one night stand with that beautiful lady isn't such a bad idea at all. You can do it and no one will know it'*.

But the truth is, God knows it and He sees it. He also expects that you discipline your body into submission under the guidance of the Holy Spirit (1 Corinthians 9:27).

When the devil perceives that the Christian has matured in faith and by God's grace is able to resist these temptations through prayer and the empowering of the Spirit, he turns the heat up. He then brings to mind some of the things you had done in the past and makes you relive it. If you were struggling with alcoholism, he will bring back memories of the times you were drunk and had so much fun with friends; but never the times this affected your family and the damage it had on your life. If you had struggled with pornography, he will bring to remembrance some of the scenes you liked and he will make you relive the feeling of a false and exaggerated sense of pleasure; but never the experience of how this increasingly dominated your life and affected your thinking about the opposite sex or the same sex. He wouldn't bring to memory how this also affected your relationship with God, where you felt guilty, ashamed and even distant from God. The devil's approach is always to create a false sense of pleasure that promises satisfaction, but in the end, it only leads to being shackled. This war the enemy wages can be draining to one's initial excitement and progress as a Christian. Sometimes you wish you could just wake up and forget about the past, but these memories could make your new life in Christ very challenging to live. The Christian at this stage must be prayerful, asking the Lord to cleanse their thoughts from the influence of the past. This process may take some time, but the believer must persist in the way of obedience and self-control (righteousness) and in renewing their mind with God's word. Ultimately, it is the Lord who will deliver them from these attacks of the enemy, but one must be fully convinced that they are ready to undergo change, because no one comes to Christ and remains the same.

Level 3.

At this stage, the devil will not just offer you the temptation or remind you of them, he will now forcibly implant these thoughts in your mind. These are thoughts that if mistaken, you the believer may perceive your own. Thoughts of immoral things, often out of character and leaving you to question how you could even think of such a thing. Sometimes these attacks are through dreams, creating a vivid image in your mind and giving you the impression that you had actually committed such a sin. These attacks are aimed at making you feel guilty when you are not. They are aimed at disturbing your peace of mind and affecting your sanity and joy. The danger of the attack is, it could start a dark and gloomy thought pattern if not dealt with. The more you try not to think about it, the more you find yourself actually thinking of it, making it even harder to overcome.

I believe it is with regard to this attack that the Apostle said, "*So to keep me from becoming conceited because of the surpassing greatness of the revelations, a thorn was given me in the flesh, **a messenger of Satan to harass me**, to keep me from becoming conceited. Three times I pleaded with the Lord about this, that it should leave me. But he said to me, **"My grace is sufficient for you, for my power is made perfect in weakness**.*" (2 Corinthians 12:7-9).

From my personal experience, I have found that these attacks must be nipped in the bud. Any thoughts that are not of God, I have learnt to reject them outright. Firstly, I say to myself, "these are not my thoughts and I reject them in Jesus name". I then proceed to pray about it and speak God's truth in faith over my life. Some of these attacks are fierce and persisting, hence the believer must be ready to devote themselves to prayer, even fasting to overcome it. Victory is assured in Jesus name, but at this stage, it is not an easy victory without contention.

Ultimately, we are now children of God. We have been delivered from the kingdom of darkness and Satan's bondage, but we have an enemy who will not agree to the terms without a fight; so, do not allow him to strip off your royal robes by deceiving you. Don't entertain his attacks without fighting back in prayer with the truth of God's Word. Stand on guard, be clothed in the whole armour of God and be ready to defend your right as a child of the Kingdom.

It means: Discipline and self-control

This will be discussed in the coming section – **The Royal Discipline**.

Ultimately, our adoption into God's family means far more than can ever be comprehended or discussed. The Apostle simply puts it this way when he said, *"Indeed, I count everything as loss because of the surpassing worth of knowing Christ Jesus my Lord. For his sake I have suffered the loss of all things and count them as rubbish, in order that I may gain Christ and be found in him"* (Philippians 3:8). Such is the priceless adoption we have in Christ. Nothing can ever be compared to the riches of knowing the Lord and our identity in Him.

Living In Your New Identity

LIVING IN YOUR NEW IDENTITY

Story of Celestine

While adoption is often positive for a child's wellbeing, the transition from the old identity to the new does have its challenges. A child that is legally adopted at a very young age may have little or no problem settling into the new family. On the other hand, older children with knowledge of their past life and experiences may find it difficult to fully engage and embrace the new change. Often this challenge arises from the process of having to fit into a new household culture that may be different or alien to what one is used to. As adopted children of God, we may experience a similar struggle as we transition from our old identity to the new. This is normal and expected, but the believer must be aware of their new identity and be intentional in making that transition.

Through the years, I have been privileged to have travelled to various countries on humanitarian or international development related work. In 2010, I was in Nairobi, Kenya located in East Africa. Kenya is a beautiful country with some amazing wild life and culture, but it is also a country marked with high rates of HIV infection and AIDS. Among other factors, the disease has left many children orphaned with some having to live on the streets.

While working there, I encountered a few of these street kids on my way home from work. They often surrounded me with their hands stretched out begging for money. Moved with compassion, I sometimes gave them the few shillings I had and prayed for them. There was a young boy in particular who stood out from the rest. I felt within my spirit that the Lord had a great plan for him. During our usual prayer meeting in the student hostel, I was moved to pray for the orphans, the street kids and this boy in particular. I shared the prayer request with the students gathered and we all prayed. As I got to church on Sunday morning, I saw these street kids in the church. Being surprised by their presence, I asked how they all found their way to church. The Pastor explained he was moved with compassion to see them on the streets so he invited them to worship and lunch after the service. He also said he felt the Lord urging him to take in one of the boys and raise him up in a godly Christian way. This boy was about the age of eleven and his name was Celestine. To my surprise, he was the same boy the Holy Spirit impressed on my heart to pray for.

After the service, the Pastor and his wife enquired about Celestine's family background and the reason why he was left on the streets. It was claimed by his uncle that since his mum died, his dad had struggled to care for him. Furthermore, his dad married another woman who wanted nothing to do with him. Being heavily influenced by his new wife, he neglected him. Additionally, his uncle claimed to be financially incapable of caring for him, and for that, he was happy for the church to take that responsibility.

Subsequently, Celestine was given a place to sleep in the shelter of the church building with caretakers watching over him. The Pastor and his wife ensured he had daily food prior to leaving the church premises. Finally, Celestine had new change of clothes from his dirty tattered shorts and shirt he had worn for months, if not years. He now wore clean and decent clothes as seen in his new shirt and trousers. On his feet, he no longer wore the worn-out slippers with large holes underneath, indicating its years of excessive use! He now had the choice of slippers, casual shoes or a smart shoe, depending on the occasion. Furthermore, Celestine was now enrolled in a government school. He was however placed in a class that was years behind his age due to his low literacy level.

Identity Crisis

Days after Celestine had been taken in, I saw him with the same group of friends begging on the streets. This time he had a new look about him, as seen in his hair cut, new t-shirt, trousers and shoes. His clothes looked clean in comparison to his friends who were unfortunately still dressed in the same tattered clothes. They approached me for money with Celestine leading the way, as he perceived I would recognise him and favour him among the rest. Sadly to his surprise, I expressed my disappointment and told him to go straight to the church. Although he could not fully understand English, he clearly understood my expression and the immediate need to go to the church. I personally marched him to the church located nearby and asked why he was still begging on the streets. I initially thought he was hungry and had resulted to the only way he knew how to satisfy his hunger (street begging). I was however told he had just had his second meal and was yet to have his dinner which was almost ready. This was confirmed by others who also claimed to have seen him eat a plate full of cornmeal mash[3] with fish. At this point, I was left perplexed by his actions because I could not understand why someone would still go out and beg on a full stomach. I told the caretaker to firmly warn him that I would not want to see him begging on the streets ever again.

Days after this incident, here was Celestine still begging on the streets. It seemed he was not having much luck, considering he looked well off in comparison to the others. Immediately he saw me, he turned the opposite direction and started running back to the church pretending he was just passing by. In spite of that, I was glad he now perceived his actions were wrong. A few weeks later, I enquired about Celestine's general wellbeing and behaviour. I was told he was a quick learner and was showing some good improvements in his studies. His teachers

---

[3] Also known as Ugali in the local language. This could be compared to mash potatoes in the UK or US.

however reported that on a few occasions he had not bothered to show up to school or return from break; but there was good news, as this behaviour was gradually curbing. This report was an obvious indication he was *bunking* off school to spend time begging on the streets with his friends. It was surprising to me that one would prefer sitting in the scorching sun, rather than be in the safety of a classroom with friends and an adult present. The caretaker also claimed Celestine often sneaked out of the church, spending hours on the streets without anyone knowing his whereabouts.

Even though the Pastors and caretakers had done all it took to improve his wellbeing and standard of living, Celestine was still living in his old identity of being a street kid, but now, a well-dressed and presented street kid! The change had occurred, but the poor boy could not comprehend the extent of the change.

Similarly, as Christians, we may sometimes feel like Celestine. We have been adopted into God's family but we may still be living the life of our old nature. The truth is, we are not street kids anymore; our adoption makes us princes and princesses through Christ.

After months of patience and daily mentoring, Celestine is now a young boy who spends his days in school, his afternoons playing football with new friends, and his evenings in the church. Gradually, he made the transition into his new way of life, which is his new identity.

Relating to Celestine's story

We can all relate to the story of Celestine in one way or another. Even though he was not adopted, he faced the struggle of having to make a transition from his old lifestyle into his new identity. Similar to Celestine's experience, we can all agree that when we came to faith it took a while to adjust to kingdom principles.

Example[4]: I woke up one day and all of a sudden I couldn't engage in binge drinking and wild parties anymore. What! No way! My old nature decides it will not go down that easy without a fight. Covertly, I resolve to visiting some party friends who did not know of my new found identity in Christ. After having a few drinks, my alarm bells started ringing, indicating I might be getting drunk. Being aware of my extraordinary dance moves under the influence, and the overly confident personality that often gets me in trouble, I say to myself, no more. Another friend buys the next round of drinks without asking if I wanted one, considering this was the usual practice among the group. I am now left with two choices; get drunk or face the scorning of friends. I chose the former and ended up being carried home by my friends!

The next day, I woke up with a hangover mixed with feelings of guilt and shame. With one hand on my head and several failed attempts of trying to figure out how I got home, I received a video message of the previous night's antics. Unable to bare the sight of what I was doing or saying under the influence, I remembered my commitment to Christ and decided to pray, asking for forgiveness in repentance. I said, '*no more of this binge drinking lifestyle for me; I want to live a life that brings you honour and praise*'.

A few days later, my old nature starts calling for some fun. What can I do for fun as a Christian? Certainly not binge drinking! I decided to go to a night club with a few friends. As I danced to the music, I realised I was now more sensitive to the revolting words in some of the songs being played. Besides, the night was not as fun as I anticipated. '*Am I growing too old for clubbing? Everyone else appears to be having fun apart from me. What is happening?!*' The Holy Spirit then whispers and

---

[4] This story is made-up to help the reader understand the process and struggle of transitioning from the old identity to the new in Christ.

says; *'you now have a new identity; the old self is gone and the new has come. You must learn to walk in this newness of life'*.

After a while, I realised I was becoming more sensitive to sin, having little or no pleasure for some of the things I used to do. As a Christian, this is evident the Holy Spirit dwells in you, indicating you are now governed by a new order of life which is of God. Referring to Celestine's experience, the transition has taken place. You cannot remain in the old nature anymore because of its discomfort. You must embrace your new identity. To be found in Christ is to undergo change, similar to the process of adoption. If you are an adopted child of God, you will become enlightened to the fact that you are not of this world anymore but of a heavenly citizenship (Philippians 3:20). If for years you have claimed to be a Christian, and you are still living the same life of sin, it is time to acknowledge your new identity in Christ and start walking in the newness of life. To this end, Apostle Paul exhorted the church of Colossae and the surrounding regions, stating;

*"If then you have been raised with Christ, seek the things that are above, where Christ is, seated at the right hand of God. Set your minds on things that are above, not on things that are on earth. For you have died, and your life is hidden with Christ in God. When Christ who is your life appears, then you also will appear with him in glory. Put to death therefore what is earthly in you: sexual immorality, impurity, passion, evil desire, and covetousness, which is idolatry. On account of these the wrath of God is coming. In these you too once walked, when you were living in them. But now you must put them all away: anger, wrath, malice, slander, and obscene talk from your mouth. Do not lie to one another, **seeing that you have put off the old self with its practices and have put on the new self, which is being renewed in knowledge after the image of its creator"* (Colossians 3:1-10).

Living a victorious life of overcoming past sins and habits is an indication of one's transition into their new identity in Christ Jesus. Then again, is the process of sanctification[5] or righteous living the only indicator suggesting one's new identity? No! There are many other factors to consider. For example: If you believe you are a child of God and your citizenship is of heaven, then why live a life of constant fear and worry? Isn't God the Almighty your Heavenly Father? Isn't Christ your Good Shepherd? Isn't the Holy Spirit your Comforter and Friend? Why fear? Why feel as though you are alone? Why feel as though no one cares?

On account of these, many believers may still be living under the old nature (old identity), whereas they are submitting to the Holy Spirit with evidence of righteous living. Some believers may overlook this psychological area of their lives and remain satisfied with their new identity. I would encourage them by saying, *sons of the kingdom, God has more in store for you than just righteous living*. There is a higher knowledge of one's identity, which is that of faith and the understanding that you belong to the family of God. It is the knowledge of faith where you know that your Heavenly Father cares for your wellbeing and that it is in His perfect will to take care of you as His adopted child. Sometimes, we may find ourselves in a similar place like Celestine, who while being assured of daily provision and protection lived a dual life of a street kid and a homed child. As adopted children, we should always have faith in our Father, not just believing He cares when all is well but also holding on to this same truth in challenging times.

The truth of the matter is; life's trials and challenges does not make you any less of an adopted child of God. It doesn't make you less of a heavenly citizen and a royal priesthood (1 Peter 2:9). This becomes an issue when we allow such challenges to cloud our thinking and

---

[5] **Sanctification** – The Greek word translated "sanctification" is the word (hagiasmos) which means "holiness." To sanctify means "to make holy." To sanctify is to set apart a thing or a person for its proper or intended use. The process of sanctification will therefore mean, being set apart to live a fulfilled life in righteousness and love as God intended us to.

perception of who we are in Christ and who God is to us (a loving Father).

It is when we are confronted with serious issues in the area of our health, finances etc., that the old nature, aroused by the spirit of fear creeps in, and the whispers of doubts become louder.

"Are you really a child of God? Does God truly love you? Why are you suffering this much if God cares for you? God is taking too long, do as you please!"

The spirit of fear gives birth to a lack of faith, which subsequently resuscitates the nature of your old identity. When fear creeps in and your faith in God is at its lowest, that is when the old nature is strengthened. It is at this point that some believers may act like Celestine, knowing that they are under a new order, yet they go back to the old ways of gambling and hoping to win some money to change their circumstances. Some may even make excuses and find good reasons to justify this, explaining that, *"if I win, I can then tithe, help the poor or give some money to the church"*. Unfortunately, while this option may appear as an overnight solution, it often opens doors to deeper financial problems if one's hope is solely dependent on it. This is not to criticise anyone reading, it is rather a reflection of my past experiences prior to growing in my faith and truly understanding my identity in Christ.

It is also in these times of uncertainty that the devil may give a list of justifiable reasons why a young mother to be, should contemplate abortion. He may whisper,

"You know he will not be there for the baby, do you want to be a single mother?" To others he may say, *"Be wise, you already have three kids, having these twins could mean you cannot afford a better life for any of them"*.

Nevertheless, for any of these reasons, we know we have a Heavenly Father who is compassionate and more than able to provide for those children. As Christians, we must trust in His love and grace because He is faithful in spite of our failings and weaknesses. We are well aware of the stigma attached to a Christian bearing children outside of marriage. While God does not approve of any other environment then marriage to raise children, He is still merciful and gracious to the single mother or young unwedded couple. This grace is not to approve of the lifestyle, but it is rather a reflection of who He is. Have faith at all times, since your Father has not adopted you to abandon you. He may delay and your circumstances may even look desperate, but your Father is able to turn it all around in just a moment.

These are but a few examples of the old nature taking precedence over the new. Referring to the case of Celestine, you must also make that full transition into your new identity, which is a child of God and a child of the light. Consider this saying, *"light cannot mix with darkness"*. In reality, it is impossible to have both elements present at the same place and time. Light always casts out darkness, and darkness never overcomes light, unless of course an object obstructs the source of light and leaves a shadow behind. God is the source of all light, and your faith in Christ Jesus could be seen as the channel by which this light shines upon you. The presence of fear and unbelief is like an obstruction to that light, leaving you in its shadows. The domain of darkness thrives in environments of fear, unbelief and worry. If the devil can hold you bound by these elements, you may never fully walk in the newness of life which is your new identity in Christ.

On the other hand, the newness of life in Christ thrives under the order of faith and total trust in the Lord. God is calling His children to assume their identity as adopted sons, having an unwavering faith and confidence in their loving Father. Such faith that chooses to trust and obey God in all circumstances. It is such faith whereby you may find your ship sinking under the battering waves and storms of life, and still have confidence in the Lord to rescue you. It was with such faith that David said, "*Though an army encamp against me, my heart shall not fear; though war arise against me, yet I will be confident*" (Psalm 27:3). This is the faith where in the gloomy scene of imminent sinking, the Lord clearly says, "*jump into the raging waters and swim to land because I am with you*". It is this faith that will not rather pray for the vessel to miraculously fix itself, or even beg God for a new vessel to come by and rescue them rather than jumping into the waters as the Lord had instructed. This is also the faith that does not consider the natural elements or the impossibilities, knowing that with God all things are possible. This is the faith of a child of God, a Kingdom Citizen. It is in explaining this new order of belief that the Lord Jesus said;

*"Therefore I tell you, do not be anxious about your life, what you will eat or what you will drink, nor about your body, what you will put on. Is not life more than food, and the body more than clothing? Look at the birds of the air: they neither sow nor reap nor gather into barns, and yet your heavenly Father feeds them. Are you not of more value than they? And which of you by being anxious can add a single hour to his span of life? And why are you anxious about clothing? Consider the lilies of the field, how they grow: they neither toil nor spin, yet I tell you, even Solomon in all his glory was not arrayed like one of these. But if God so clothes the grass of the field, which today is alive and tomorrow is thrown into the oven, will he not much more clothe you, **O you of little faith?** Therefore do not be anxious, saying, 'What shall we eat?' or 'What shall we drink?' or 'What shall we wear?' For the Gentiles seek after all these things, and **your heavenly Father knows that you need them all**. But seek first the kingdom of God and his righteousness, and all these things will be added to you*" (Matthew 6:25-33).

Jesus was not saying that we will not face life's challenges as children of God. He was rather calling us to realign ourselves to His truth, taking off the blindfold restricting our vision of God's love towards us. It is a call to take off the ragged clothes of constant fear held together by the devil's deceptive belt of lies. It is a call to cast off his jacket of rejection that has no place in your heavenly royal wardrobes anymore. Take off those blindfolds, take a good look at yourself; why should an adopted child of God, a Heavenly citizen, remain dressed in fear, constant worry, unhappiness, all kinds of stress, hopelessness and sin? This is not your identity in Christ. In faith, put on your new identity as a child of God and start walking in this newness of life.

Your Identity And Kingdom Ministry

YOUR IDENTITY AND KINGDOM MINISTRY

"Children are a gift from the LORD*; they are a reward from him"*. (Psalm 127:3) *New Living Translation.*

With the rising number of single parents in modern society and the challenges associated with raising children, not a lot of people will (*although some will*) leap for joy when the pregnancy test shows that sign, (I)—you are pregnant. But the truth of God's word still remains, *"children are a gift from the Lord"*. Some may look at them suckling on their mum's breast and may only perceive their cute tender and feeble frame, but deep within that very child may lie the seed of a great president, an inventor, a teacher, a doctor, a sports person, the breakthrough for AIDS and cancer etc. This is the gift from the Lord, yes, that child is that very gift to the world.

Similarly, as Christians, there were gifts the Holy Spirit deposited in us when we were born of the Spirit and adopted into God's family. Each child of God carries a gift entrusted to them for the building of the church and the expansion of God's Kingdom influence on earth. Similar to how a rough dry seed with no particular significance or beauty, has within it the ability to sprout into a beautiful flower or a fruit tree, is how a new believer has within them the ability and gifts to blossom into a great vessel of honour for the Lord. We have spiritual seeds of giants and gladiators embedded in many believers of our generation. Some do not know this of themselves yet, while others are preoccupied with the things of the world, only setting enough time aside to spectate rather than fully engage in battle. To these giants, I believe the Lord would say; *"Arise and take your place in the church, being found completely clothed in the armour of God and ready for action"*. To others who may feel they do not have much to offer in the church, be encouraged because you are of much worth. You are the church, the bride of Christ, the light of the world and the salt of the earth. You carry God's presence and influence with you. You are that light of hope that shines in your home. You are the fragrance of God that gives off the pleasant smell of joy and encouragement at your work place. You are the church of God and could be the only voice that speaks to the heart of that young girl or boy heading in the wrong direction. You are a gift to the world and of great worth to the Kingdom.

Who would have known that a speech by a fisherman could see over three thousand people confess faith in the Lord? That fisherman was Peter, an Apostle of the Lord. Such is the power of the gift entrusted to us. Who knows, that homeless addict across the street could be a great evangelist to the nations. Do not underestimate the power of the Gospel and the gifts of the Holy Spirit to transform lives. Every soul has a place and a service in the Kingdom, so be inspired by this and use your gifts to the glory of God.

Identical identities of believers

There are diverse gifts for various services and activities in the church; all are empowered by the Holy Spirit for the common good of building the church of God (1 Corinthians 12:7). This diversity is however displayed in an identity that all believers share in. Seeing through the lenses of the Spirit, one can even perceive this majestic privilege conferred upon some pauper in the poorest country in the world. This privilege Christians enjoy is that;

1. We are all children of God i.e. children of the King (1 John 3:2).
2. We are all servants and stewards of God (1 Corinthians 4:1-2).

Our identity as children of God

As a Christian, it is such a privilege to be called a child of God. This identity is both humbling and exalting, in that we must all come to Christ in humility, acknowledging our inadequacy to attain God's righteousness. It is in our humility and acknowledgment of what Christ has done, to which we are exalted by adoption as children of God. The billionaire and the pauper will both enter by grace through faith in Christ alone, and one day, they will both bow before Him indicating that God is not a respecter of persons (Romans 2:11; Acts 10:34).

Psalm 62:9 states, *"Those of low estate are but a breath; those of high estate are a delusion; in the balances they go up; they are together lighter than a breath"*.

This passage gives us a glimpse into how the Lord perceives all mankind irrespective of their race, wealth or social status. On this basis, the world's richest man is no different from a pauper, since they both must repent, trust in Jesus and humbly follow Him as Lord and Saviour. Furthermore, the identity they both share as children of God brings a sense of equilibrium and brotherly love, where dignity, respect and humility is observed as a result of this identity. The pauper is no longer identified by his lack of material possession but by his true identity as a child of God. Likewise, the great rich man is no longer identified by his wealth and earthly status, since his true identity is a child of God and a brother to the pauper. It is to this truth that Apostle Paul rightfully said in Romans 3:27,

"Then what becomes of our boasting? It is excluded. By what kind of law? By a law of works? No, but by the law of faith."

By this revelation of one's true identity in Christ, all racial or cultural pride or antagonism is done away with. The one who may feel inferior because of their race is now elevated in Christ to the status of a child of

God. The one who takes pride in their racial identity or conceived superiority over others, is humbled by the truth that in Christ such superiority does not exist; all are sons of God by grace and not by works. Again, if we had any worldly pride or achievements to boast about in relation to faith, it is excluded in Christ by grace, since we are all one big family of princes and princesses who owe their identity to God's grace and nothing of themselves.

What it means to be a child of God

Being a child of God chiefly speaks of our relationship with Him. It speaks of a strong peculiar affection, expressed in love, compassion and acceptance of us as His children. This love is both strong and tough in discipline, yet also tender and considerate to our weaknesses. In this love, we have a promise that He will not leave us nor forsake us. This is an assurance that He is with us in all circumstances, both good and bad, our Father is with us and will see us through. In this relationship, we have a provider, a protector, a healer, a comforter, a friend etc.; but we also have in Him a just, a holy and a sovereign God. It is imperative to understand that through Christ, we have come into fellowship with the fullness of God. We did not just receive a God of grace, mercy and love, but we have come into fellowship with the fullness of His nature and being, which includes His righteousness, holiness, sovereignty etc. In His whole essence, this amazing God has chosen us as a people for His own possession (1 Peter 2:9). This implies that as His children, we have a strong binding relationship with Him, enabling us to fellowship with our Father in a more intimate way. Through this relationship, we are assured we belong to Him, enforcing our identity as His sons.

As a teenager, I worked in a popular retail store that sold clothes and accessories. I was employed as a customer service person for the men's department as well as for the women's shoe department. During our seasonal sales, we often had hundreds of people visiting the shop on a daily basis. In the midst of the chaos, you may hear an announcement made citing a code that corresponded to a 'missing child'. The procedure was that the child was kept in one department, while an announcement was made for their parents to make their way to that department. The child who at this point could be crying is assured that his or her parents will be there soon. Often, the reason for this assurance is that we know they **belong** to a particular family who are equally desperate to be united with them. It is in acknowledging the binding relationship between that child and their parents to which we assure them of this truth. In its simplest sense, we are saying, 'little child, you are not abandoned because you belong to someone who loves you and will not leave you'.

Similarly, our relationship with God through Christ is far more binding than any other earthly relationship we have known. This relationship is not easily broken or severed, even when it seems we are forgotten, forsaken, rejected and abandoned. The covenant truth still speaks over every child of God, you are His treasured possession, being heirs of an everlasting inheritance with Christ Jesus. Our identity as sons therefore speaks of our belonging and relationship with Him, as expressed through birth right or adoption.

Our identity as servants and stewards of God

Our identity as servants and stewards looks at our role and duty within the Kingdom. We have been adopted as children not only to receive cuddles as babies while sitting in the safety of the palace, but rather with the expectation to mature and take responsibility in furthering the Kingdom's influence on earth. It is important to note that we were not only adopted for duty; we were first adopted as sons but there is much work to be done in the Kingdom.

One of the most inspiring passages I have found on this topic is a subtle scripture that is often overlooked but conveys much truth to the fact that we are all called and equipped to serve in the Kingdom. Sometimes as believers, we are our worst critics. A reflection of our self and our high view of others could mean we exaggerate our weaknesses and inadequacies, creating the perception that others are better suited for service than us. On the other hand, some may feel that their participation in serving the church could be demeaning to their worldly reputation, but this notion is far from the truth when one is enlightened by the awe of who they have been called to serve.

A service to her majesty the Queen is perceived as a noble task for which one takes pride in performing. Even a cleaner in the palace, if permitted, will proudly say to all that they render such service to the Queen. This pride is rooted in the identity of who the service is rendered to, thereby vanquishing any feeling of self-deprecation. Now consider who we have been called to serve and never feel ashamed, but take all pride in serving His awesome majesty the King of kings and Lord of lords.

A great example of this was an experience I had in my previous job in a church based in Croydon UK. During my time of ministry in that church, I took on a brief role that meant I worked closely with the accounts department. I was granted an insight into the finances of the church, seeing who gave regularly and how much they gave. To my surprise, the highest giver was a humble lady who was equally passionate about serving. She could be seen in the kitchen serving tea and coffee, tidying and washing up, putting chairs away, as well as praying with others for their needs. This came as a shock to me because one could never have imagined that someone earning that amount of money could humble themselves and serve the church in such capacity. This was both inspiring and humbling, as it demonstrated a heart that has been transformed by the Gospel and a mind that perceives the honour and greatness of who is being served.

Some reading this may feel that they don't have much to offer in service to the church or the Kingdom. As a challenge to this notion, the Apostle said, "*To each is given the manifestation of the Spirit for the common good*" (1 Corinthians 12:7). Note that the Apostle did not claim the manifestation of the Spirit was only for **some**, or was working through **some**, but rather, "**to each** *is given the manifestation of the Spirit for the common good*". This implies that every believer has been given a gift empowered by the Holy Spirit for the common good of building the church and advancing God's Kingdom on earth. But what does this gift or the manifestation of the Holy Spirit look like?

For many Christians, their perception of the gift and manifestation of the Holy Spirit is overly spiritualized when they hear of prophecy, healing or speaking in tongues etc. Instantly, many rule themselves out because they find it inconceivable to be used by the Lord in such a way. But despite this feeling, the word still stands; "**to each** *is given the manifestation of the Spirit for the common good*", meaning you are also entrusted with a gift. You may feel inadequate, but our God is sovereign, impartial, full of compassion and full of grace. This implies, He does as He pleases, He uses whom He chooses irrespective of who they are; and above all, He gives the grace and power needed to fulfil the calling. The issue here is therefore not the type of work or the gift needed, but rather the faith to unlock available vessels who are willing to be used in such an awesome way.

With that said, the gift of the Holy Spirit and its manifestation need not be only spiritual, although it is spiritually empowered. In Romans 12:6-8, the Apostle details some of what the manifestation of these gifts are. In this passage, he said,

"*Having gifts that differ according to the grace given to us, let us use them: if prophecy, in proportion to our faith; if* **service**, *in our serving; the one who teaches, in his teaching; the one who exhorts, in his exhortation; the one who* **contributes**, *in generosity; the one who leads,* *with zeal; the one who does acts of **mercy**, with cheerfulness"* (Romans 12:6-8).

Additionally, the Apostle also included **helping** and **administrating** to this list in 1 Corinthians 12:28. Straightaway, we can note that those who contribute generously to the church are also a gift. It is the same Spirit working in the prophet that also works in the generous giver's heart, urging them to be a good steward of the resources entrusted to them. You may find some members who are not exactly well to do, but they are generous with their finances. This is a gift to the church and it is not a delightful burden that we all share, although everyone is encouraged to give generously.

Again, the same Spirit that empowers the fervent preacher of the Word also empowers the person who can't help themselves but be moved with great compassion for the poor and suffering. While we are all encouraged to be compassionate to those who are less privileged; you would find that in the church we have those who are very passionate about helping the poor and suffering. You will also find others who can't help themselves but make the worries and struggles of others their own burden. According to Paul, this is a unique gift to the church where some individuals are more empowered and filled with the compassion of Christ to show incredible acts of mercy.

In my experience prior to pastoring, although I knew I had been entrusted with the gift of teaching and preaching, I somehow found myself helping in various departments of the church. I couldn't seem to sit still when help was needed. I found myself on the sound and visual team, floor managing team, intercessory team, small groups team, evangelism team, admin team, youth team etc. Why did I do this? I really don't know why, but I simply felt the need to help. In Paul's letter, this is also a unique gift to the church where some people are empowered with the skills and passion needed to serve in the various departments. These people may probably not lead any of the departments but they are entrusted with satisfactory skills to generally serve across the board.

From these examples, it is clear that the manifestations of the Spirit are much broader than we could imagine. The Holy Spirit works in an individual by using his/her natural gifts as well as imparting or depositing evidently spiritual gifts in them. What I mean is, your sound technician in the church probably didn't have to be prayed for to receive the knowledge of tuning and mixing music. He probably knew how to work on a PA system before coming to faith. Likewise, the caterer who may organise food for church events probably had the skills of cooking and managing a group before they got saved. The difference therefore lies in who the service is rendered to, and how the Holy Spirit works in the believer's heart to faithfully serve in this capacity. In understanding this, we can say that the Holy Spirit works in such a believer by sanctifying their natural gifts. On the other hand, there are the evidently spiritual gifts that no amount of money or natural ability can enable one to function in. These are the gifts of prophecy, healing, discerning of spirits etc. So, while the Holy Spirit empowers all the gifts in the church, some are **Sanctified Natural Gifts** and others are **Evidently Spiritual Gifts**. Understanding this manifestation of the Holy Spirit in the church is so refreshing, as it means we all have something entrusted to us for the advancement of the Kingdom.

In this book, I will refer to both the Sanctified Natural Gifts and the Evidently Spiritual Gifts as gifts of the spirit, since they are all spiritually empowered but mainly because the Bible does not make a distinction.

Being used by the Holy Spirit

The Holy Spirit is the third person of the Trinity. He was present in creation (Genesis 1:2), His power gives life to that which is created, (Psalm 104:30) and eternal life to those found in Christ Jesus (Romans 8:11; John 6:63). A key part of His work is to empower the saints for ministry in the church and for the advancement of the Kingdom. This empowerment is essential for all believers because Christ didn't even start His public ministry without the clothing of the Holy Spirit (Matthew 3:16-17). Likewise, the Apostles were told to wait in Jerusalem until they were clothed with the power of the Holy Spirit (Luke 24:49) before they should venture to fulfil the great commission. It is undeniably clear that a Christian life of ministry is impossible without this empowerment. But is this empowerment a unique experience that is similar to what happened on Pentecost? Or is it a subtle indwelling of the Spirit upon confession of faith or baptism? The position I take is, we all receive the Holy Spirit on confession of faith, since one cannot confess true faith in Christ without the work of the Spirit (John 6:44; 1 Corinthians 12:3). However, from my personal experience, I am equally convinced that the Holy Spirit grants believers a unique extraordinary experience of being filled with His power as a testimony of His work in them (Ephesians 5:18).

Some of the attributes of our God is that He is sovereign but He is also not the author of confusion (1 Corinthians 14:33) i.e. He does things orderly and not carelessly. By His sovereign and orderly attribute, the Holy Spirit empowers believers for ministry in two main ways. The first is by **spontaneous supernatural gifting** and the second is by **specialisation of gifts.**

Spontaneous supernatural gifting

From scripture, we acknowledge that the Holy Spirit carries the power of God. It is by His infilling that mere men were empowered to do extraordinary things. It was by His power that Peter and John said to the crippled man, *"I have no silver and gold, but what I do have I give to you. In the name of Jesus Christ of Nazareth, rise up and walk!"* after which the crippled man started walking (Acts 3:6).

The power of the Holy Spirit is immeasurable, since He is the same power that created and also gives life. The Bible states that as believers our bodies are a temple of the Holy Spirit (1 Corinthians 6:19); meaning, the Holy Spirit of God is now pleased to dwell in us because in Christ we are children of God. If the Holy Spirit now dwells in us, then we are confident we can be used in every capacity and in every way according to His will. In light of this truth, we can also lay our hands on the sick and pray, and by faith, speak healing and the sick person will be healed. We can all receive prophetic words from God to speak God's revealed truth to others. The Holy Spirit can also use any of us to interpret a tongue (be it earthly or spiritual) as a way of edifying the church. Ultimately, we can be empowered with every gift for ministry because the gift giver Himself (the Holy Spirit) dwells in us.

I have called this type of empowerment, **spontaneous supernatural gifting**, since it rests on the sovereignty of the Holy Spirit working with the faith of the believer to accomplish an immediate will of God. The sovereignty of the Holy Spirit means; He empowers any believer He wills with any gift He chooses for God's Kingdom purposes. This would suggest that if a believer has faith to pray for the healing of another, by understanding their identity and the authority in the name of Jesus, the Holy Spirit can supernaturally empower them with the gift of healing as they pray for that person.

I have witnessed a case where the Holy Spirit supernaturally used a lady during prayer to powerfully prophesy in church. Her words were to the lead elder who at that time needed much encouragement due to the challenges the church faced. This lady was shaking on her knees as she prophesied with tears streaming down her face. It was a unique experience to behold, one that was instantly discerned as the Lord speaking to Him. It was uncommon for her to speak in such a way, and during my whole time in that church, it was the only time she prophesied.

This spontaneous supernatural empowerment is not something that happens on a daily basis, since by the sovereign will of the Holy Spirit, He may also decide not to act at that moment. Ultimately, while we embody the Holy Spirit, He is not obliged to act at our command or in relation to the desires of our heart. He only does so when our faith is in line with His will to serve the purposes of God. Then again, while it rests on the sovereign will of the Holy Spirit to act, He does so through available vessels with faith. This simply means, if you ever want to see someone get healed by your prayer, you must be willing to step out in faith and pray for people. You may face some disappointments, but by God's will some will be healed. If you want to prophesy, earnestly desire it and pray about receiving that gift. One must be intentional and prepared to receive words (or even images that come to mind) from the Holy Spirit. One must also be confident and bold in speaking forth these words. But as I stated before, it is not by man's assertion or will that the spontaneous supernatural gifts of the Holy Spirit are given. It is only by the sovereign will of God to serve His purposes.

Specialisation of gift

While we can believe God for the spontaneous supernatural gifting of the Holy Spirit, the overwhelming scriptural evidence points to specialisation of gifts in the body of Christ (the Church). In Apostle Paul's letters to the churches in Rome, Ephesus and Corinth, he described an orderly functioning of gifts in the church, one that can be compared to how the human body functions. In addressing the topic of spiritual gifts, he said, *"The human body has many parts, but the many parts make up one whole body. So it is with the body of Christ* [the Church]*"* (1 Corinthians 12:12; New Living Translation). Again, he reiterated this in Romans 12:4-5 (NLT) as he said, *"Just as our bodies have many parts and **each part has a special function**, so it is with Christ's body* [the Church]. *We are many parts of one body, and we all belong to each other"*.

Symbolically speaking, the Apostle is saying that the Holy Spirit empowers the functioning of the church like the human body. The human body is made up of many parts, some internal and others external, but all these parts function together as one body. According to the teaching of the Apostle, each person confessing faith in Christ was baptised into His body (1 Corinthians 12:13) with the aim of functioning like a specific organ or a limb. Each organ in the human body has a specific function; meaning in the church, the Holy Spirit empowers us with specific gifts to function in different capacities and departments within it. In explaining how the Holy Spirit positions and empowers each person for ministry, Paul said,

*"To each is given the manifestation of the Spirit for the common good. For to **one** is given through the Spirit the utterance of wisdom, and to another the utterance of knowledge according to the same Spirit, to another faith by the same Spirit, to another gifts of healing by the one Spirit, to another the working of miracles, to another prophecy, to another the ability to distinguish between spirits, to another various*

kinds of tongues, to another the interpretation of tongues. All these are empowered by one and the same Spirit, who apportions to each one individually as he wills" (1 Corinthians 12:7-11).

From this scripture, we can note an orderly apportioning of gifts in the church. To one is given through the Spirit the utterance of wisdom and to another the gift of healing etc., indicating a specialising function of gifts in the church. Ultimately, although we all possess the immeasurable indwelling power of the Holy Spirit, it is clear that He sovereignly empowers us with specific gifts to function in specific capacities within the Church.

Then again, does the Holy Spirit empower us to be useful in just one area of ministry? Not entirely, since I previously explained how the Holy Spirit empowered me to serve in different departments of the church. Additionally, I occasionally get prophetic words and dreams detailing things that will happen in my life or in the lives of others. In my previous church, I participated in outreach events and street evangelism, and I was told by a few people that I appeared to be naturally gifted in this area. The question then is, does receiving prophetic words and being 'a natural' evangelist make me a Prophet and an Evangelist? No, I am neither a prophet nor an evangelist, since my true gift is in teaching and preaching God's Word. I personally do not feel called to evangelism (called as in having the gift of an evangelist), and although I may appear confident to others on outreach, it is an area I personally find slightly challenging to function in. This challenge is neither based on preference nor comfort, but rather it is simply down to the fact that it is not my area of strength. Alternatively, if I was asked to prepare a sermon to preach to an audience, although the topic may be challenging and I may not be the most eloquently spoken person, this calling however comes natural to me. Hence, while I may appear to do well in evangelism and may occasionally receive prophetic words and dreams, my **dominant gift** is actually in teaching and preaching God's Word. You may also find others who may breathe and live evangelism, even having a gift of healing to go with it, but then they may find it tough to prepare and share topical sermons in a church setting. This revelation brings a fresh understanding of what the Apostle meant by specific gifts and functioning in the body of Christ. Specialisation of gift need not be perceived as only one gift or function per person. It should rather be viewed as a proportion of gifts with a dominant area, enabling speciality and alternating. I have below, an illustration of what I believe my allocated gifts are, including my dominant gift. Note that this is just an example, as this does not include all my gifts or accurately depict each area.

Diagram 1: Christopher Eke's gifts with dominant gift

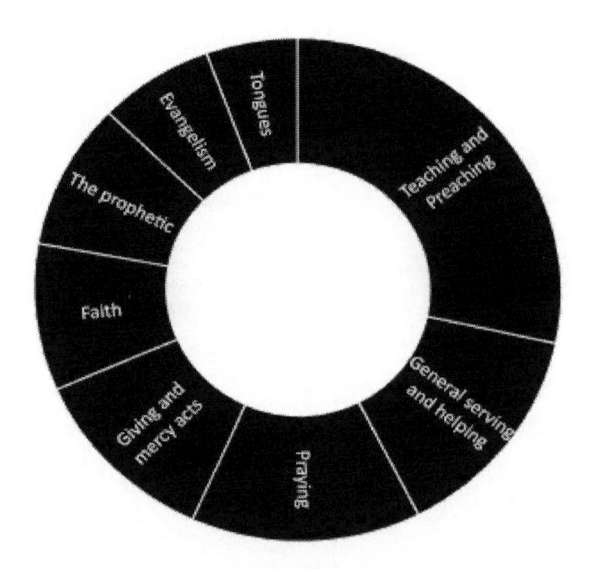

From the diagram, you can conclude that while I may occasionally be moved to show acts of mercy or even support our church outreach, nothing however moves me more than spending time preparing a sermon to share with the church.

This idea of specialisation and proportional gifts could be compare to a football team. In a football game, each player varies in their ability and footballing skills. Some are good at dribbling, passing and scoring. Others are very pacey, able to defend and offer short and simple passes. Some have incredible stamina, running continuously from their defence only to terrorise the opponent with pin-point crosses in their box. All these players can run and kick a ball, but the variation in their ability and skills mean each player has a dominant area of strength. In this area of strength, one sees themselves as a striker, the other a winger, another a midfielder and then a defender and a goal keeper. While a striker may be urged to go back and defend if necessary, he will however not function as effectively as playing in his natural striking position. This challenge highlights the importance of specialisation within the team, with each player functioning in their dominant ability and strength. A key observation in a football team is that, no player works in isolation but rather all work as part of a team that displays a sense of dependency on each other. The world's greatest striker is no good on the pitch alone. While he may have the ability to score a hat-trick, this is only made possible by his dependence on other teammates to supply him with a good pass. Equally, without the defence, though he scores a good goal, his team will end up losing with no one to protect their end of the goal.

In a similar notion, the Holy Spirit has apportioned specific gifts to each member to enable specialisation, alternating and interdependence. In a wholesome church, you will find in it the Pastor and elders, the prophets and evangelists, the treasurers and administrators, the worship leaders and musicians, the children and youth workers, home group leaders, helpers, generous givers, cleaners, sound and media team members etc. A good pastor cannot do everything, nor can anyone else do everything. The Holy Spirit has placed all these gifts in the church to spread the burden and enable the church to function effectively. In highlighting the importance of equally honouring every gift, the Apostle said;

"For the body does not consist of one member but of many. If the foot should say, "Because I am not a hand, I do not belong to the body," that would not make it any less a part of the body. And if the ear should say, "Because I am not an eye, I do not belong to the body," that would not make it any less a part of the body. If the whole body were an eye, where would be the sense of hearing? If the whole body were an ear, where would be the sense of smell? **But as it is, God arranged the members in the body, each one of them, as he chose. If all were a single member, where would the body be?** *As it is, there are many parts, yet one body. The eye cannot say to the hand, "I have no need of you," nor again the head to the feet, "I have no need of you."* **On the contrary, the parts of the body that seem to be weaker are indispensable, and on those parts of the body that we think less honourable we bestow the greater honour, and our unpresentable parts are treated with greater modesty, which our more presentable parts do not require. But God has so composed the body, giving greater honour to the part that lacked it, that there may be no division in the body, but that the members may have the same care for one another**." (1 Corinthians 12:14-25).

In summary, this section of the Apostle's letter speaks of the fact that God is not the author of confusion, indicating that the Holy Spirit functions in an orderly fashion to bring harmony and unity to the many members that belong to the one body of Christ (the Church). In so doing, He gives poise and honour to every functioning member of the body; meaning, there is nothing like an undignified gift or service in the church. From this, we understand that the cleaner is equally important to the preacher, since they all belong to one body, only differing in function. Ultimately, a good understanding of the Apostle's teaching brings a sense of satisfaction and contentment in one's apportioned gift and service in the church. It is clear that even though we may have proportionally allocated gifts with a dominant area, there are however some other gifts that we do not have. The Apostle is saying that this is quite normal and expected in the church, but rather than mourn or express jealousy over our neighbour's gift, we should rather be content with what we have and be focused on using and developing our dominant gift. Equally, being content does not imply one should remain a church caretaker (for example), when that person senses an emerging gift of prophecy entrusted to them. Though the Holy Spirit positions us in specific departments, we should also be opened to His sovereign repositioning or reequipping for other ministries. In recognising this truth, Paul wrote, *"But earnestly desire the higher gifts. And I will show you a still more excellent way"* (1 Corinthians 12:31). There is therefore a need for contentment, as well as a yearning for more of what the Holy Spirit has for us.

Then again, there is sometimes an unhealthy pressure and expectation for believers, mostly pastors to know it all and do it all i.e. have all the spiritual gifts and its manifestation. This notion is far from the truth, since according to scripture the Holy Spirit does not empower us to function in every area of the body. In addressing this misconception, the Apostle asked,

"Are all apostles? Are all prophets? Are all teachers? Do all work miracles? Do all possess gifts of healing? Do all speak with tongues? Do all interpret?" (1 Corinthians 12:29-30).

The obvious answer to this is: **no Apostle, we don't all do it. Some have a dominant gift in one area but lacking in another.** A clear example of this truth is seen in scripture, when after the Holy Spirit had used Philip the evangelist to perform great miracles in Samaria, Peter and John were sent to lay their hands on them to receive the infilling of the Holy Spirit (Acts 8:14-17). The question here is: Why was Philip unable to do this when he had already cast out demons from some of the locals? Some may say he just wanted to honour the Apostles, but I believe it simply comes down to the fact that this was not his area of ministry; or plainly speaking, he did not have the authority or gift for this ministry. Again, Paul was used in a mighty way to preach the gospel and to heal the sick. In Acts 14:8-18, we are told of how the Holy Spirit used him to heal a man crippled from birth. But then, in his letter to the church in Galatia, Paul explains he was ill (body aliment) when he first visited the church in Galatia to preach the Gospel (Galatians 4:13-14). He also hints at how this affected his ministry but then claimed he was encouraged by the way the church received him. Again the Apostle said in 2 Timothy 4:20, "*Erastus remained at Corinth,* ***and I left Trophimus, who was ill, at Miletus***". The question is: why did the Apostle leave Trophimus ill at Miletus? From this we know that his dominant gift was not in healing, but rather in being an Apostle entrusted with preaching and teaching the Gospel. This also indicates that while the Lord may use a Man of God in an awesome way to heal others of their sicknesses, they themselves are not supernaturally shielded from ill health.

You may see some ministers who place themselves on a pedestal of invincibility, teaching that as a Christian one of God's promises to us is to have good health at all times. On the day they fall ill, you will either not see them in church or when they do turn up, they will call it a spiritual attack of the enemy! You may also find others who are *well to do*, claiming they are traveling on holiday but actually, they are travelling to receive medical assistance in another country. Why raise the standards so high and then live a double life when God sovereignly does nothing?

Anyway, the main point is, we have all been entrusted with specific gifts in the body of Christ. Each person's gift put together is the jigsaw that completes the whole puzzle. It is by recognising our strengths and seeing what we are lacking as a strength of others, to which we can function as one unified body. Ultimately, the purpose of specialising and ministering in one's dominant gift is to build an excellent church. If all ministers in their strength, the church will be a glorious one. You are a unique gift to the church, so be encouraged to use what is entrusted to you for the glory of God.

Your Identity And The Question Of Your Salvation

YOUR IDENTITY AND THE QUESTION OF YOUR SALVATION

What is salvation? Salvation is the act of saving, protecting or rescuing someone (or people) from harm, suffering or distress. In Christianity, salvation is seen as the act of being saved from the imminent wrath and punishment of God as an ultimate consequence of sin. In every story of salvation, there is a saviour who does the act of saving. In the Christian faith, this Saviour is Christ Jesus. According to scripture, His death on the Cross was the perfect sacrifice that atoned for our sins and appeased the wrath of God. If our sins are therefore atoned for, having been nailed with Christ on the Cross then surely, we must be saved. Well, even in the most confident of confessions, some Christians still battle with the lingering thought of – am I truly saved? Or will I go to Heaven or Hell for the sins I keep committing? These are questions that many believers would want answers to, and while there is the objective truth that Christ died to save sinners, there is also an underlining truth that if we deliberately continue in sin, we will not inherit the Kingdom of God (Hebrews 10:26-29; 1 Corinthians 6:9-10). This poses a challenge for many, as we are all aware of our weaknesses and failings. As a result, some are left to ask the question; am I saved by faith in Christ only or does what I do affect my salvation? Since we are not all perfect, we are therefore bound to sin sometimes. The question is, will this sin affect your salvation? And if not, how can you live a genuine Christian life that is worthy of the calling without abusing God's grace?

This section of the book will present the reader with various scriptures that wrestle with this topic, but ultimately aims to build within them a heart of repentance, a reverence for the Lord and the confidence in understanding their adoption as children of God.

Is it once saved, always saved OR am I being saved, for which I have a part to play in its completion? Which one is it?!

This is arguably one of the most frequently asked question in the church. It is a question that has caused much intense discourse and division among believers, yet after over two-thousand years the church is still no closer to an agreement. A simple reason for this is because the Bible presents the reader with scriptures that suggest both arguments to be true, depending on one's interpretation. In my opinion, these passages are not contradictory or opposing to each other; they are rather parallel truths that speaks into a believer's life at different stages of their life. In the book of Hebrews, it is written, *"For the word of God is living and active, sharper than any two-edged sword, piercing to the division of soul and of spirit, of joints and of marrow, and discerning the thoughts and intentions of the heart"* (Hebrews 4:12). If the word of God is living and active, then we know that these parallel truths are there to speak into our hearts at different stages of our lives. What I mean is, God's word will speak hope of eternal salvation into a sinner's life, but His word will also point the sinner to repentance or face the natural or eternal consequences of sin.

Example: In February 2015, I volunteered in a project aimed at the less privileged and homeless. The project was in partnership with a group of churches that opened their doors to the homeless during the winter season. The church provided them with a warm place to sleep (the church building), hot food to eat, hot shower and a change of clothes. This was a temporary solution until the council could find them a place to stay. Through conversation, it became clear that some of the people were made homeless due to some bad lifestyle choices. Others were homeless because they lost a job and had struggled to keep afloat with rent payments, bills etc. The general notion was that, most of these people have had a tough time and hence the project was there to treat them with dignity and respect, as well as offering them the warmth and care they didn't usually get outside the doors. As I engaged one of the men in conversation, it was obvious he was a substance abuser. He had blamed his environment for the way his life had turned out. To him, it seemed people didn't care about him, even his friends and family deserted him when he needed them the most. As we spoke, a Bible laid on the desk next to us. He picked up the Bible and randomly flicked to a page and started reading. To my surprise, this was the passage he read;

"save yourself like a gazelle from the hand of the hunter, like a bird from the hand of the fowler. Go to the ant, O sluggard; consider her ways, and be wise. Without having any chief, officer, or ruler, she prepares her bread in summer and gathers her food in harvest. How long will you lie there, O sluggard? When will you arise from your sleep? A little sleep, a little slumber, a little folding of the hands to rest, and poverty will come upon you like a robber, and want like an armed man" (Proverbs 6:5-11).

After he read this, there was the awkward moment of silence while he gently placed the Bible down. I thought to myself, God has a sense of humour! But the truth is, God's word is living and active and it spoke directly into the life of the man who appeared to blame everyone else but himself. If he would only obey the word of the Lord, the remedy was not only that Jesus saves, but the specific word for him was to take responsibility for his life and repent from a lifestyle of laziness. So, while God's word may have encouraging messages of hope and joy, it also has the corresponding truths of rebukes and warnings to enable us live a life worthy of the calling.

On the other hand, regarding salvation, the only challenge with using this view is that, there is a strong objective truth stating we are saved by grace through faith in Christ; but there is also the subtle truth that deliberate sinning has a certain or even an uncertain eternal consequence for the believer who persists in it, but an assured consequence for the unbeliever.

This section will explore some of the thoughts of what scripture teaches on this important topic of our identity.

Once saved always saved

This is a biblical teaching that places emphasis on the finished work of Christ on the Cross. The centrality of the Christian Gospel is the message that Christ died to pay the penalty for sin and to reconcile us to God. If our sins have already been paid for and we have now been reconciled to God, then in Christ we are at peace with God. In this view, when a sinner comes to faith, all their sins (past, present and future sins) are forgiven. Some believers may even go as far as saying; no matter what you do, the finished work of the Cross still assures your salvation by your faith in Jesus. Is this saying scripturally true? We will examine if this belief has any basis later in this chapter.

Additionally, Christ died on the Cross over two-thousand years ago, meaning, even before you were born or could even have conceived sinning, Jesus died for your sins. This leads us to a few conclusions;

1) The work of the Cross was completed in spite of us, although it was for us.
2) The work of the Cross was completed while we were still in sin.
3) We could never have deserved it or even earned it because it was done before we were born and before we knew what sin was.
4) In light of these truths, we can conclude that our salvation is by sheer grace.

Apostle Paul puts it wonderfully as he says, *"For by grace you have been saved through faith. And this is not your own doing; it is the gift of God, not a result of works, so that no one may boast"* (Ephesians 2:8-9).

If we are saved by God's grace (God's unmerited favour) as a gift through faith in Christ, then surely our actions (sinful nature) have nothing to do with receiving a gift that is purely unmerited (not determined by our actions aside of our faith).

Again, to reiterate this point, the Apostle wrote to the church in Rome and said;

*"for all have sinned and fall short of the glory of God, **and are justified by his grace as a gift, through the redemption that is in Christ Jesus, whom God put forward as a propitiation by his blood, to be received by faith**. This was to show God's righteousness, because in his divine forbearance he had passed over former sins"* (Romans 3:23-25).

As we examine these passages, we see the same key words (grace, gift and faith) being used to explain how we are saved in Christ. As if these weren't overwhelmingly gracious, Paul goes further to claim how this salvation and justification is not a result of works but a result of faith. In his letter to the church in Rome, he wrote,

*"For what does the Scripture say? "Abraham believed God, and it was counted to him as righteousness." **Now to the one who works, his wages are not counted as a gift but as his due. And to the one who does not work but believes in him who justifies the ungodly, his faith is counted as righteousness**, just as David also speaks of the blessing of the one to whom God counts righteousness apart from works: **"Blessed are those whose lawless deeds are forgiven, and whose sins are covered; blessed is the man against whom the Lord will not count his sin."*** (Romans 4:3-8)

With reference to these passages, it is clear that our salvation is a gift from God received by faith in Christ. Additionally, according to Paul, we are justified and counted righteous by faith and not by our works. If it were by our works, it would not be a gift, it would rather be our due.

Having established the basis of our salvation, some may still ask the question: *"Now that I am saved, can I lose my salvation?"*

This is a simple but also a tough question to answer because as believers, we have the objective truth that Christ saves sinners by grace through faith. On the other hand, there is also hidden information regarding an individual's personal life and walk of faith. This hidden information makes it harder to generalise this truth even though the objective truth can be pronounced over them on the basis of their faith. With the challenge this poses, we can try and answer this question with an illustration of how scripture claims we are saved. According to scripture, we are saved by;

1) The gift of God's grace **IN** Christ through his atoning death for our sins.
2) Our faith **IN** Jesus' atoning death for the forgiveness of our sins and justification for our righteousness.

The basis of our salvation is simply illustrated as follows:

Diagram 2

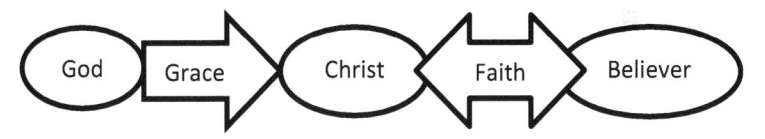

God → Grace → Christ ← Faith ← Believer

From the illustration, God's gift of grace is only found **IN** Christ alone. In other words, Christ embodies God's grace and He is the free gift of God given to us. On the other side, a sinner can only receive this grace by having faith **IN** Christ. Having faith as in, believing in who He says He is (the Son of God), and believing in what He said He came to do (lay down His life as a ransom to give eternal life to all who will believe). Many theologians however express that the initial faith a person has in Christ is God given, hence the arrow of faith pointing in both directions. This means, no one can come to faith without the work of the Holy Spirit or without God initiating it. However, man also has a responsibility to respond to this faith that has been awoken in them.

From this illustration, we can conclude that God's grace and the gift of eternal life is deposited in Christ alone and received by faith alone. Our **faith** is therefore the bridge that connects us to God's grace and the gift of eternal life. If a believer then claims that he/she does not believe (does not have faith) in God or Jesus anymore, they then automatically detach themselves from Christ who is the embodiment of God's grace and eternal life. By the definition of these passages, where there is no faith, there remains a missing link that connects to the Saviour in whom is God's grace. Furthermore, this person that once believed in Christ can no longer identify themselves as a believer, since their Christian identity is only in connection with their confession of faith in Christ Jesus. Ultimately, without faith in Christ, there still remains hostility with God, leading to the imminent wrath and judgement of God on that sinner.

This is illustrated below.

Diagram 3

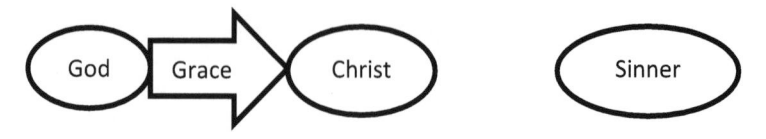

God → Grace → Christ   Sinner

In Christ alone do we have access to this grace. In Him alone are our sins forgiven. In Christ alone is the full weight of God's wrath absorbed by the sacrifice made on the Cross. If only you can take your faith to the Cross, you can then exchange God's wrath that was meant for you with God's peace and grace in Christ. It is at the Cross that we are made new creations. At the Cross, we who were once orphans are made children of God and reconciled to God; but it is all only through faith.

In contrast to this, without faith in Jesus, there is no access to God's gift of grace leading to salvation. Additionally, people of other faiths (such as in Islam) who hold the belief that they can only be saved by their good works unfortunately fall in this category. From scripture, it is clear that no one can earn God's grace and the gift of eternal life by merely observing laws or traditions.

The law is honourable and it provides us with guidelines to help us live a good moral life. The law is good for personal discipline as well as for community governance and moral upholding. On a personal level, as one observes the law, it creates a sense of righteousness (right standing with God) where their conscience remains clear and their good behaviour is approved by others. In this sense, a person can be called *righteous* or given a title of a *good* man/woman.

But in contrast, the law also convicts us of sin. It points to our guilt and failings. With the law, we will forever have a guilty conscience because we are not perfect beings and we still fall into sin. By the law, we are held accountable for sins committed, since the law is the standard for judging. Above all, observing the law does not undo or cancel out former and future sins; meaning, while we may take pleasure in our good and moral standards, we will forever be guilty of sins committed before a Holy God.

Some have tried to explain their way out of this predicament by teaching that on the day of judgement, our good deeds will be weighed against our bad deeds. If our good deeds outweigh our bad deeds, then we will enter heaven. In other words, if our sins are 49% and our good deeds 51%, that will be good enough for heaven. While this view may sound convincing to some, it leaves us with serious questions to ask.

1) It implies, you don't really have to be a good person, just do enough to outweigh your bad deeds and you are fine. This teaching is not scriptural nor is it consistent with the teachings of the Law that calls everyone to obey it at all times.

2) It could imply that one can trick or cheat the system (or even God) into entering heaven. What I mean is, in this view, you can always decide to do a lot of good deeds at will, not out of love or care for others but rather as a way of accumulating more good deeds to cheat your way to heaven.
3) The idea of judging by weighing one's good deeds against their bad is not compatible with the nature of law and justice.

Expanding on point 3

In the court of law, an offender is not judged by comparing their good deeds to their bad. Even if an offender has lived a good moral life, their transgression of the law is what they are ultimately judged by.

For example: An armed robber who is being tried for robbing a local store will not be judged by the years he committed no offense. His righteous deeds cannot outdo or cancel out the offense of armed robbery. The decision to determine his guilty verdict is not weighed up against how good he had been prior to the offense committed. The robber is found guilty on the basis of transgressing the law apart from his good deeds.

Similarly, our efforts of trying to escape God's wrath by solely observing the law or accumulating good deeds will not suffice to outweigh any past sins committed. In the presence of a Holy God, a spot or blemish of sin is far too grievous not to arouse judgement. This brings us back to the same predicament; in the law and in the righteous judgement of God, we are sinners who deserve His wrath.

The law is therefore meant to point us to Christ in whom is God's grace and mercy that leads to eternal life. In Him alone are we declared righteous and justified by His atoning death and resurrection. The saddest reality is that, the strictest adherent of the law can never outdo or undo any offense committed; they can only hope that their prayers of forgiveness may cause God to overlook their offense. But in Christ, not only do we pray for forgiveness of sin, but we also have an atoning sacrifice made for us. This sacrifice provides the Christian with a secured stance before God (not out of pride but in humility of what Jesus has done) since the believer does not only hope to receive forgiveness, but is also assured of the legal debt payment made by Christ. In comparing our justification by grace apart from the law, Apostle Paul expressed his concern for those who seek eternal life in the law by saying; *"You have been severed from Christ, you who are seeking to be justified by law; you have fallen from grace."* (Galatians 5:4) NASB.

In light of these scriptures, I am led to believe that a person can indeed lose their salvation if they became an atheist or declared unbelief in Jesus Christ.

Predestination and Election: A stronger case for once saved always saved

While the above passages and illustrations may appear to water down the case for once saved always saved, the stanch adherent to this teaching base their belief on the scriptures that claim God's sovereign election and predestination (preordained, predetermined) for salvation. Several passages in the Bible, especially in the New Testament provides the reader with strong evidence that God initiates and appoints one for salvation in Christ. Some examples of these passages are;

John 6:37, "**All that the Father gives me will come to me, and whoever comes to me I will never cast out**".
Note: It is the Father that gives us (believers) to Jesus, implying that our response to the Gospel was initiated by God.

John 6:39, "*And this is the will of him who sent me,* **that I should lose nothing of all that he has given me, but raise it up on the last day**".
Note: If it is the will of the Father that Jesus should lose nothing of all that has been given to him (believers), then we are confident that our salvation is secured, since the will of God must be fulfilled.

John 6:43-44, "*Jesus answered them, "Do not grumble among yourselves.* **No one can come to me unless the Father who sent me draws him**. *And I will raise him up on the last day*""
Note: Our response to the Gospel was not of our own doing, it was the Father that initiated the birth of faith in us and drew us to Jesus. It is therefore those who are drawn to the Lord who will be raised into eternal life.

John 10:25-30, "*Jesus answered them, "I told you, and you do not believe. The works that I do in my Father's name bear witness about me,* **but you do not believe because you are not among my sheep. My sheep hear my voice, and I know them, and they follow me. I give them eternal life, and they will never perish, and no one will snatch them out of my hand. My Father, who has given them to me, is greater than all, and no one is able to snatch them out of the Father's hand**. *I and the Father are one.*"
Note: Again, it is the Father that grants the faith to believe in Jesus Christ as Saviour. It is the Father that gives us to Jesus. Ultimately, our security in Christ is made clear when the Lord said, "*My Father, who has given them to me, is greater than all, and no one is able to snatch them out of the Father's hand*". The question here is: How could one possibly lose their salvation if the Father is determined not to let them go? Additionally, how could one possibly lose their salvation if the devil cannot even snatch them out of the Father's hand? Then again, does this passage refer only to the disciples of Christ, or does it encapsulate the truth of salvation for all believers?

Acts 13:48, *"And when the Gentiles heard this, they began rejoicing and glorifying the word of the Lord,* **and as many as were appointed to eternal life believed**.*"*

Note: The Gentiles did not believe because they liked the message of the Gospel and therefore decided to choose the new path of life. The passage is clear in stating that those who believed were stirred to faith because they were appointed by God to eternal life. A question to think about is: If God has chosen you and appointed you for eternal life, could anything sabotage His plans? I doubt it, since Jesus has stated that no one can snatch us out of His hand and the Father's hand.

Ephesians 1:4-5, *"even as* **he chose us in him before the foundation of the world, that we should be holy and blameless before him. In love he predestined us for adoption as sons through Jesus Christ**, *according to the purpose of his will"*

Note: Apostle Paul makes a profound statement here by claiming that believers were chosen to be found in Christ before the foundation of the world was established. The passage also states that we were predestined for adoption as sons through Jesus Christ. A question to reflect upon is: If God has predestined us (believers) to be adopted as sons, having fulfilled this through establishing our faith in Christ, will He then change His mind and renounce our sonship? Or could anything stop Him from accomplishing what He has predestined to do with us?

Romans 8:29-30, *"***For those whom he foreknew he also predestined to be conformed to the image of his Son,** *in order that he might be the firstborn among many brothers.* **And those whom he predestined he also called, and those whom he called he also justified, and those whom he justified he also glorified***"*.

Note: The word foreknew adds a greater significance to the passage, in that although God foreknew every human being that ever lived, the context in which this word is used points to a peculiar affection for believers in Christ. The passage explains that it was because God had predestined to save us (believers) through Christ that He called us, justified us and subsequently glorified us. It is clear that God is fulfilling His plan of salvation in us as evident of our faith in Jesus Christ.

In light of these passages, we can make the following conclusions.

1) God predestined the believer to be saved.
2) God is executing (or has already executed) this plan through the faith the believer has in Christ.
3) If God has predestined to save the believer and nothing can stop His plans, then our salvation is secured in Christ, since His grace upholds the believer's faith and sees him/her through the path of life.

These conclusions form a good basis for the teachings of once saved always saved. Furthermore, if one will choose to dispute this teaching, they may have to wrestle with the significance of Jesus' atoning death on the Cross. What I mean is, they may have to answer the question: Was Jesus' death and sacrifice on the Cross incomplete? Did Jesus die to partly save us or fully save us?

On the other hand, to take the stance of once saved always saved could perhaps imply that believers do not have freewill to make choices, which gives the impression of robots being controlled by God. If that was the case, then why haven't we become perfect beings since we became Christians? Why do we still fall into sin once a while? Can we dare to say that God has led us to sin, since He is the one who predestined to save us and is subsequently leading us in the path of life? By no means! The writer of James challenges this notion by saying, *"Let no one say when he is tempted, "I am being tempted by God," for God cannot be tempted with evil, and he himself tempts no one"* (James 1:13).

Another question that arises with this stance is the challenge of considering who is truly saved or not. If all believers are elected and predestined as evident in their confession of faith, then why does the Lord state in Mathew 7:21-23;

"Not everyone who says to me, 'Lord, Lord,' will enter the kingdom of heaven, but the one who does the will of my Father who is in heaven. On that day many will say to me, 'Lord, Lord, did we not prophesy in your name, and cast out demons in your name, and do many mighty works in your name?' And then will I declare to them, 'I never knew you; depart from me, you workers of lawlessness.'"

It is obvious that the people being referred to in the passage are Christians, since it is evident by their prophesying and great works done in the name of Jesus. Although they are believers, it is shockingly clear that not all are saved. Does this imply that believers need more than just a confession of faith to be saved? And if they are elected for salvation as evident by their faith in Christ, why does this passage speak of the Lord's rejection of some? Could this mean that among believers are found true remnants elected for salvation? And if these remnants that are elected and predestined cannot purely be identified by their confession of faith, then on what additional basis do they qualify to be saved?

The passage is however plain in pointing to the reason for their rejection as being **workers of lawlessness**. The stanch adherent to the belief of once saved always saved may say that those rejected were never truly saved in the first place. If that were the case, then what is the basis for salvation if not by grace **through faith in Christ**, since those rejected in the passage appeared to have faith in Jesus Christ as their Saviour, and yet were not counted among the Lord's chosen. These are tough questions to answer, but as the Apostle said, we are to *work out our salvation with fear and trembling*, knowing that we are elected by God and saved by His grace alone through faith alone.

The case for salvation by grace through faith as evident in a transformed heart

In Paul's letters to the churches, the Apostle was insistent in the message he preached, claiming that salvation is a gift of God's grace received by faith in Christ Jesus. Most of Paul's letters had both theological and practical teachings of faith, interwoven to provide the reader with a holistic message that cuts across every area of life. The practical teachings aimed to bring the new believer into alignment with Kingdom principles, where their confession of faith is rightly expressed in their everyday life. In other words, they do not only confess faith, but also practically live it out as children of God belonging to God's Kingdom and governed by God's Word.

In my sixth form years, every teenager was eager to pass their driving test in order to be seen in their new car. It was the years when having a full driver's license and a car placed one in the category of an elite group! Attaining this status had many benefits, including the well desired attention from the beautiful girls in that year. The recognition was instant, girls who never said a word to you may now say hi! Some may even ask for a ride, and guess what, when they jumped in your car, they came with a friend as well! It appeared this status made up for what one did not have in physical appearance, hence every young man took their driving lessons and test seriously. The driving test consisted of two parts, the theory and the practical. The theory test focused on one's knowledge on road signs, right of way, perception of hazard and general theoretical driving practices. The practical test assessed the driver's competence behind the wheel to gauge whether they can actually drive. It assessed if the driver was good enough to drive without jeopardising the lives of other road users.

To qualify for a license, neither the theory nor the practical test was good enough on its own; since one must pass both tests to be licensed. What good is it for one to have passed their theory test when during their practical test, they decide to ignore road signs and drive contrary to traffic? How does that show their understanding of road practices or prove their road worthiness? It simply doesn't; and for the examiner, it will be a relief to break the news of a **fail** to the learner after enduring such driving!

Again, what good is it for a person to own a car and drive practically safe on every road, when in reality they have no license? Even if they are the safest driver in the world, the prerequisite of not having a license makes them a transgressor of the law. Ultimately, it is in being licensed that one can express their independent quality of being a good driver.

In our pursuit of attaining a full driver's license in sixth form, a close friend of mine (Nick) was the first to book his practical test after passing his theory test. On the day of the test we were all confident he would pass, having shown us what a good driver he was. After the test, we eagerly awaited the news, but sadly, it was a fail.

This was how our conversation went.

Nick, what happened bro!?

He replied: *"Man, I wasn't comfortable driving with both hands [on the steering wheel] so I decided to drive with one hand and the other on the gear stick!"*

I asked, why would you do that in your test?

He replied: *"I wanted to prove I got skills man!"* In other words, I wanted to convince the examiner I am a good driver even with one hand on the wheel. (This is something to avoid in a driving test if you want to pass).

What! What else did you do wrong?

He replied: "*A few cars were slowing me down so I overtook them*". What he actually meant was, he was over speeding during his practical test!

I don't know if it was his immaturity or sheer foolishness, but his actions cost us our legitimate ride and his license. In light of this, the examiner could never have passed him because although he scored good marks in this theory test, he did not demonstrate the same knowledge practically.

In a similar notion, Paul wrote to believers who were baptised in water and some filled with the Holy Spirit, sternly warning them that those who believe (Christians) and yet make a practice of sinning will not inherit the Kingdom of God[6]. In 1 Corinthians 6:9-11, Paul said:

"*Or do you not know that the unrighteous will not inherit the kingdom of God?* **Do not be deceived**: *neither the sexually immoral, nor idolaters, nor adulterers, nor men who practice homosexuality, nor thieves, nor the greedy, nor drunkards, nor revilers, nor swindlers will* **inherit the kingdom of God**. *And such were some of you. But* **you were washed, you were sanctified, you were justified** *in the name of the Lord Jesus Christ and by the Spirit of our God.*"

Note that prior to mentioning some of these practices, Paul said, "**do not be deceived**"! In other words, he meant, do not be misled or fooled. Why would the Apostle make such a comment to believers who are baptised, filled with the Holy Spirit and predestined for salvation? How can they be deceived if God's grace upholds them? His choice of words may imply that, for a believer who may have misunderstood the message of grace and its power to save from sin, there could be the presumptuous notion that the deliberate practice of sinning could have no effect on one's salvation. Indeed, this same idea is now evident in

---

[6] Using the phrase: *In a similar notion*; is not to say that Christians must pass some test in order to be saved. We are saved by God's grace in Christ Jesus through faith alone.

many churches today, where sin is rampant and sexual immorality is considered too sensitive a matter to address. In some churches, all a believer may have to do is to confess Jesus as Lord, be baptised, attend church services a few times, tithe, and then they are on their way to Heaven. But the message is shockingly clear; **"do not be deceived"**, those who practice these things will not inherit the kingdom of God.

Then again, despite the stern warning of verse 9 and 10, some readers of this letter could possibly develop a false permissible notion in verse 11, claiming that although these sinful acts are true for some believers, they are however washed, sanctified and justified by faith in Christ. This interpretation may give a false sense of freedom in Christ, which for some, could wrongly be seen as a license to live as they please. Is this what Paul meant? I doubt it! Let us read the passage again.

1 Corinthians 6:11, "*And such **were** some of you. But **you were washed, you were sanctified, you were justified** in the name of the Lord Jesus Christ and by the Spirit of our God.*

The Apostle was intentional in using past tense when referring to the practices he believed some of the readers were involved in. Why use past tense even though these practices were a present reality in the church? I believe Paul was calling them to re-examine their new identity in Christ and align themselves in accordance to this truth in a practical sense. His statement, "*And such **were** some of you*", clearly points to the fact that a transformation had taken place, implying that the believer must no longer be comfortable living a life of sin. In other words, Paul is saying to the readers:

*Brothers and sisters, don't you know who you are in Christ? You were once living the life of sin (verse 9 and 10), but in Christ, you are now an adopted child of God. The life of sin is of your old nature [such **were** some of you], you must now align yourself to your new nature of* *righteousness and holiness, since you have been **washed, sanctified** and **justified** in Jesus Christ.*

Paul knew that the best way of communicating the Gospel in a practical sense was to ensure that the believers understood their new identity in Christ. If the church in Corinth could only see beyond the worldly perception of who they thought they were (a worldly identity shaped by their culture and society), to now perceiving the truth of their actual identity as children of God, only then will they conduct themselves accordingly. Obviously, just like some of us, these believers needed a few reminders, but eventually, this new identity became a part of their nature. To this end, Paul knew that understanding one's identity was far more important than teaching *do's and don'ts*. *Do's and don'ts* can sometimes be meaningless without a clear grasp of identity or purpose.

Example: Have you ever been in a job where you were always told what to do but never really understood why you did it? There was always a sense of fear that if you did not do what was expected, you could be fired. While this is true for most jobs, the experience of working in an environment where one feels insignificant without any true sense of belonging, is far worse than being fired. Eventually, that person may perceive their job as mere routine, always looking forward to lunch at 1pm or home at 5pm. Working in such an environment with **'a do as you are told'** management style, often leads to a lack of job satisfaction with no sense of belonging. But if you were given a job title with some description of how your work contributes to meeting the organisation's (or department's) targets, you may then have a clear sense of purpose, significance and identity found in your work. You will then do your job, not out of the fear of being fired, but rather out of understanding the responsibility and significance your job conveys in helping the organisation.

Similarly, Paul knew that if he could get the church in Corinth to understand that they were actually now adopted children of God and royal priesthoods, his rebuke of such lifestyle would no longer be seen as a mere call to adhering some moral practices; it would rather be a question of identity – **Don't you know who you are in Christ?** The question of identity is personal; it carries a sense of worth and meaning to why the believer should now practically live their life in the way of the Lord. This identity is not what you are told to do, but rather who you are. It is your inner most being (Christ in you, The Holy Spirit in you) springing forth from within you and engaging with others on a daily basis.

In contrast, the *do's and don'ts* approach is often impersonal for the recipient of the message (i.e. *"Do this and not that, or else …… would happen to you"*). Even though this approach is sometimes necessary for warning or rebuking, in most cases the recipients may not fully comprehend why they are actually doing what was asked of them. They may do it anyway for fear of consequences, but essentially, it is somewhat meaningless without true comprehension. Nevertheless, in using this approach in Christ, we understand that we do not have the spirit of fear, but of power, of love and of self-control (2 Timothy 1:7). Based on this truth, Apostle Paul preached the message of grace, calling unbelievers to the gift of adoption in Christ and believers to a deeper understanding of their identity as children of God.

Having briefly established the context in which Paul made these statements (in verse 11), the message still remains; "**do not be deceived**", those who practice these things will not inherit the kingdom of God. Why? Because you **were** washed by the precious blood of Jesus, you were sanctified by the Holy Spirit and you are justified by faith.

You were washed: If a person has been washed clean by God's grace in Christ, why should they return back to that which made them dirty in the first place? The idea of returning back could be compared to the story of Celestine who after being taken in by the church, should decide to put aside his new clothes, put on his old dirty tattered clothes and return back to sleeping on the streets. Even if Celestine only did this once a while, it would still be perceived abnormal to anyone. While the problem of sin can in no way be compared to having a bath, changing clothes and not sleeping on the streets, believers are being encouraged to pursue a life of purity by submitting to the will of the Holy Spirit. The act of washing is a spiritual reality of the transforming power of God's Word, when one listens to a preach or reads the Word of God. The Word of God is the water that washes the conscience of a believer, challenging their thoughts and empowering them to pursue purity and righteousness in Christ. In the book of Ephesians, the Apostle describes the act of washing by saying, *"that he might sanctify her, having cleansed her by the **washing of water with the word**, so that he might present the church to himself in splendor, without spot or wrinkle or any such thing, that she might be holy and without blemish"* (Ephesians 5:26-27).

Ultimately, the Word of God is Jesus Christ (John 1:1; John 1:14) and He is the one who washes us. To this end, the Apostle is exhorting the believers to remain transformed by the knowledge of Christ (The Word of God), rather than being conformed to the passions, trends and lifestyle of this world. We were washed, and are being washed by the Word of God because we belong to the Bridegroom (Jesus Christ). What a joy to know that the Lord desires us; however, the aim of His washing is to present to Himself a bride (a church) that is spotless and without blemish.

Every marriage requires purity, affection and unreserved dedication and respect for one's partner. It is for this that we have been washed and set apart for the Lord. Yielding one's self to the pleasures of sin after being washed by the knowledge of Christ can be compared to a married person whose heart and affection is bent towards another lover. They are committed to the marriage for the sake of convenience and the recognition, but they also don't mind falling into the other lover's arms once a while. It is to such promiscuousness that the Apostle warned the church by saying; *"**Do not be deceived**"*! The Lord ransomed you, and for that He deserves your unreserved affection, dedication and respect.

You were sanctified: This is a positional truth explaining that when we came to faith, we were made saints, made holy and pure. This expression is a condition of the heart, mind and soul of a Christian. It is in calling believers to align themselves to this truth that Apostle Paul said;

"Do not be conformed to this world, but be transformed by the renewal of your mind, that by testing you may discern what is the will of God, what is good and acceptable and perfect" (Romans 12:2).

In renewing one's mind to the truth of sanctification, the knowledge of being a saint becomes personal and practical. A believer that understands their identity as a saint will not be comfortable living a lifestyle of sin. Persisting in this lifestyle can be compared to the story of Celestine, who although being taken in was still begging on the streets or even worse perhaps stealing from local shops. He did this despite having all the food he could eat provided by the church. It is obvious the young man's mind had to be renewed to the truth of his new identity. This alignment eventually took place after the Pastor and caretakers persisted in mentoring him and explaining he did not have to beg or steal anymore. Similarly, as we are progressively sanctified by the Holy Spirit through the enlightenment of God's Word, we are to come to the knowledge of renewal, where we can practically live as liberated saints who are free from living a life of sin.

You were justified: The term *justified* could also mean vindicated. To be vindicated implies, to be cleared or acquitted of an offense, blame or suspicion. To be justified also means to be declared righteous on the basis that one has now been acquitted of the charges against them. Being justified in Christ is one of the amazing works of God's grace, in that, while we were guilty of sin, Jesus paid for our sins and vindicated us from the charges brought against us. Through this vindication, we have been declared righteous before God.

The question then is: If we have been vindicated by grace, why then return to committing the same offense that brought the charges in the first place? We were vindicated from the guilt of an overwhelming debt we could never have paid. We were vindicated from severe charges that are punishable by death (physical and spiritually eternal). Above all, our vindication was not of our own doing, but of the unmerited favour of a merciful, righteous and all-knowing Judge. Having been vindicated by the mercy and grace of this Judge should clearly arouse a repentant heart transformed by this mercy. This does not mean a Christian will live a perfect life after receiving this knowledge of grace, however it does mean that after receiving such mercy, the believer's heart is transformed and set on bridling themselves away from sin.

Let us use a short scenario to explain this:
Imagine an armed robber was caught in the act of robbery and arrested. In the law of the land, armed robbery is punishable by death on the cross. In court, all the evidence provided presented a solid case that the offender was guilty and must be executed. In spite of the incriminating evidence, the judge (who was also the king) wanting to show compassion and still remain impartially righteous, made a decree that if there was found one innocent person in the land who was willing to take the death penalty in place of the offender, then he will be set free.

As the decree went out, it became apparent that no one was innocent in the land. All were guilty of various offenses and wouldn't even dare to come forward lest they also die with the offender. Searching the records, there was one who was found to be blameless and holy. It was a name registered to the palace; the only son of the judge; a prince of the land and heir to the throne. One of the king's servant searching through the records said to himself, "*He is righteous and meets the* criteria, but a prince can never be a candidate. It is preposterous to think that a prince should be humiliated, bearing the agony of crucifixion; and all for a guilty armed robber to be free?! Ha-ha! No chance of that happening".

On the day the final verdict was to be read, the Judge sat on his seat in the presence of the offender and witnesses. He read the charges against him, and made a final call for any innocent person willing to take his place. The room was silent for a few seconds, and then the door flung open. Walking in was the king's only son, dressed in his royal robes. As he came in, he embraced the armed robber in the presence of all, and said to his father, *"I will take the place of this man. Please set him free, for he has a wife with three children who desperately need him"*. The king, knowing that this decree cannot be annulled, turned his face aside with a heavy heart and a trembling hand gripped on the gavel. His only son (the prince) heard the decree and has freely chosen to face the death penalty for a guilty armed robber. In silence, the nation watched as the gavel was struck on the sounding block. There was an instant exchange of places. The innocent prince became the guilty robber to face the death penalty; while the guilty robber took on the innocence of the prince and was then vindicated. In the presence of all, the executioners came in and stripped the now guilty prince off his royal robes, scourging him as they led him away. The king and the now vindicated armed robber followed closely behind, seeing how others joined in to humiliate his son as he carried the weight of the cross he was to be hung on. With tears in his eyes, the king turned to the robber and said, *"That was meant to be you, not my son"*. Eventually, the prince was nailed to the cross and was hanged for a crime he never committed. The king saw his only son crucified. The nation saw the prince humiliated and crucified. The armed robber who was now vindicated also saw the prince stripped off everything (naked), beaten, scourged, spat on and crucified for a crime he did not commit.

The knowledge of such grace and the sight of beholding the prince hanging on the cross *with his blood dripping for a crime he did not commit*, is more than enough to transform the heart and mind of anyone; especially the vindicated armed robber. To behold such mercy and sacrifice and deliberately continue in a life of crime, is to look at the cross in contempt and mock the sacrifice made for one's freedom.

Similarly, to continue in deliberate sinning after coming to the knowledge of Christ is to look at the Cross in contempt, mocking the one who laid down his life for ours. Ultimately, it is not that one has not been vindicated of the charges of sin, but rather, their heart condemns them; for they neither show remorse, nor do they repent, but they have looked at the Son of God humiliated and crucified for their sins and yet they have deliberately turned aside to do the very thing that cost Him His life. It is to this that the Apostle rightfully said; **"do not be deceived"**, do not be fooled, because God is righteous, He is an impartial judge and He will judge righteously. He knows the very depths of our hearts. He sees us as we are and knows our thoughts. He knows those who have seen the Son of God crucified for their sins and have been transformed by it. He knows those who have repented upon seeing their affliction laid on the Lord and have turned from the life of sin. He knows those who have seen the Son of God bleeding for their sins, and although not there yet, are daily working out their salvation with fear and trembling (Philippians 2:12). He also knows those who have looked at the Cross, seeing what great sacrifice was made for them, yet have belittled it. They have used their freedom in Christ as a license to deliberately sin, while confidently claiming an appreciation for the sacrifice made by Christ. Regarding this, the writer of Hebrews said,

"For if we go on sinning deliberately after receiving the knowledge of the truth, there no longer remains a sacrifice for sins, but a fearful expectation of judgment, and a fury of fire that will consume the adversaries" (Hebrews 10:26-27).

Does this suggest that we are saved by our works? Not at all! We have already established from the previous sections that we are saved by God's grace through faith in Christ.

In his book, **Generous Justice**, Timothy Keller wrote about the type of faith that saves, saying; "*We are saved by faith alone, but not by a faith that remains alone. True faith will always produce a changed life*". In other words, if the faith we profess has heaven's authority and power to make us children of God, then this same faith must have the power to transform our lives and our very nature. The truth is, God's grace has the power to save us from His wrath on sinners. His grace in Christ pardons our sins and bears with our weaknesses. However, God's grace goes beyond all of that, taking root in one's life and utterly transforming that person. It is His grace that gives us a new identity as adopted sons, not only in professing but as evident in lifestyle. If one claims to be saved by God's grace through faith and that person is still swimming in the filth of sin, then I would say as the Apostle said, "**do not be deceived**", God's grace will never leave you the same way it found you. His grace has made you a child of God now, a royal priesthood, a heavenly citizen, a slave to righteousness and a temple of the Holy Spirit. By renewing your mind with these truths, one can clearly perceive why a Christian cannot remain comfortably bound by the habit of lying, stealing, sexual immorality (fornication, adultery, homosexuality and sex with animals), anger, drunkenness etc., because God's Spirit in that believer will challenge them to submit to the new order of things. But then again, will the Spirit of God continually contend with a believer's heart that is deliberately bent on practicing sin or justifying such practices?

Example 1: You may find someone who confesses to be a Christian, but at their work place they are comfortable taking bribes or using deceitful means to extract money from others. Such practices are very common in many Sub-Saharan African countries, where you may find some believers presumptuously saying; '*God understands because it is the* *way of life here'*. It is obvious that such a heart has muted the voice of the Holy Spirit and has chosen to deliberately live contrary to God's righteous standards for selfish gains. Having embraced this type of lifestyle, should God then change His standards; knowing very well the amount of people being affected by this practice? Should God then turn a blind eye to such behaviour, just because the person professes to be a Christian? I believe not!

Example 2: You may find another believer or even a preacher who is openly gay (a practicing homosexual) and proud of it, one who is happily comfortable with who they believe they are. Having taken such a stance, it is obvious that God's voice of reasoning and call to repentance is deliberately ignored, having been blocked out by pride and self-justification. Some may say, *'why repent for loving another? If God loves me, it is only right that I am able to express my love for my partner'*. Others may say, *'I cannot help it, God created me this way'*. With these supposed convincing arguments, it is plain that God's word concerning this matter has no relevance to them at all.

It is with regard to this misconception of God's grace in Christ that Paul wrote to believers (saved by grace through faith) in Galatia saying;

"Now the works of the flesh are evident: sexual immorality, impurity, sensuality, idolatry, sorcery, enmity, strife, jealousy, fits of anger, rivalries, dissensions, divisions, envy, drunkenness, orgies, and things like these. ***I warn you, as I warned you before, that those who do such things will not inherit the kingdom of God****."* (Galatians 5:19-21)

As believers, we must understand that God is not mocked, that's to say, He is not blind, nor is He fooled by anyone. Jesus paid a heavy price for our sins as He took on the full weight of God's ultimate wrath upon Himself. On that basis, we are forgiven, redeemed and justified through Christ not as a result of our works. However, to look at the Cross and behold our Saviour crucified and bleeding for a death that we deserved, and still remain unrepentant, untransformed, and even defending a lifestyle of sin while encouraging others to do the same, is evident of a heart of a thug and a rebel, not a heart of a son who appreciates the sacrifice paid for his adoption. There is a clear difference between a believer who understands he has sinned and repents knowing that God will forgive Him; to another who confesses to be a believer and yet deliberately sins without any sense of remorse while also justifying himself by his own faith. Concerning this, the writer of Hebrews wrote;

"For it is impossible, in the case of those who have once been enlightened, who have tasted the heavenly gift, and have shared in the Holy Spirit, and have tasted the goodness of the word of God and the powers of the age to come, and then have fallen away, to restore them again to repentance, since they are crucifying once again the Son of God to their own harm and holding him up to contempt. For land that has drunk the rain that often falls on it, and produces a crop useful to those for whose sake it is cultivated, receives a blessing from God. But if it bears thorns and thistles, it is worthless and near to being cursed, and its end is to be burned." (Hebrews 6:4-8)

In God's Kingdom, there is always room for the repentant heart that receives God's grace by faith and humbly walks in appreciation of the sacrifice made by Christ. On the other hand, there is no room for rebels, meaning unrepentant believers who deliberately choose to rebel against God's word. If there was room for unrepentant rebels, then Satan would have been the first chief rebel to be restored. Additionally, on the day of judgement, if a deliberately sinning believer is pardoned after belittling the sacrifice made by Christ, how could God be just in condemning others who rejected Christ and continued in deliberate sin? They have all done the same, only that one confesses to be a Christian and the other doesn't. In light of this, will just confession be enough when the heart remains unrepentant? I doubt it, because God knows the depths of our hearts and He knows those who have been transformed by the knowledge of the sacrifice made by the Saviour.

Having come to this conclusion, I encourage believers to be confident and secure in their adoption, since God is loving and has not adopted us to later abandon us. He has predestined and called us to be adopted as sons, and no one can sabotage His plans. But I will also say as Peter said; *"Therefore, brethren, be even more diligent to make your call and election sure..."* (2 Peter 1:10). This is not to say that after receiving God's grace, we are to turn to dead works in an effort to strive and complete what is already finished by the Lord. It is rather a call to examine ourselves to see whether we are still in the faith (2 Corinthians 13:5).

Based on this truth, I will preach the Gospel and confidently assure a sinner who repents of their eternal security in Christ. Nevertheless, I cannot discern the condition of anyone's heart, hence I will also preach of God's righteous judgement on sin. After extensively encouraging the church of the innumerable riches and treasures in Christ, Paul the Apostle still found it necessary to warn believers against the practice of sinning. If the core message of Paul's letters is full of grace, having its roots in the finished work of Christ, yet incorporating stern warnings against sin, how could I (or any other preacher) then preach anything less!

Are you saved as a Christian? **Yes, you are! Even adopted as a son.**

Can you fool the Lord by your confession of faith while you remain unrepentant and in sin? **No! God is never mocked! He sees the depths of your heart, for which no man (not even your Pastor) can answer for you.**

The Royal Discipline

THE ROYAL DISCIPLINE

The Royal Standard

"For the moment all discipline seems painful rather than pleasant, but later it yields the peaceful fruit of righteousness to those who have been trained by it." (Hebrews 12:11)

The writer of Hebrews used the word painful (or in the King James Version: **grievous**) to describe the feeling of undergoing discipline. The process of discipline is not the most pleasant experience, since it often means that one will have to adhere to some strict practices in order to attain a certain goal. This practice could be the act of training oneself in a sport such as boxing, which requires the painful commitment of daily fitness training, strict diets and mental preparedness. The discipline of most successful sports men/women ensure they are up in the gym very early in the morning while others are still asleep. The question is: Do they prefer to be up early, while they have the desirable alternative of lying in bed? Or do they prefer to work twice as hard in the gym and yet be the last to leave the gym? I believe the answer is No! However, for one to be known as the best in any sport, they will have to painfully discipline themselves to attain the standard of invincibility. In explaining this type of discipline, Apostle Paul said; *"Every athlete exercises self-control in all things. They do it to receive a perishable wreath, but we an imperishable. So I do not run aimlessly; I do not box as one beating the air. But I discipline my body and keep it under control, lest after preaching to others I myself should be disqualified"* (1 Corinthians 9:25-27).

The mention of disqualification is often uncomfortable with many Christians, as it may lead to a notion of being justified by our works rather than grace through faith in Christ. Others may also perceive the notion of disqualification as implying that the believer may not receive a reward from the Lord (Revelations 22:12) at his return, as opposed to losing one's salvation. Refer to the section: **Your identity and the question of your salvation** for my views on this topic.

From the Apostle's statement, it is however clear that self-discipline is essential in our Christian walk and calling. Giving the scenario of being adopted into the Royal Family, how does this type of discipline play a role in our story? One may note that despite all the riches, honour and social status the royals enjoy, their lifestyle of self-discipline is truly a painful one. Being part of the family places one at the pinnacle of society, where they are expected to be the epitome of what is noble and right.

In a world where there is the freedom of lifestyle choices and freedom of speech, not a lot of people will say much to the fact that they may have seen their next door neighbour excessively drunk on a night out. However, no one will expect to see a royal prince/princess in such a drunken state, paralysed by alcohol and being helped on their feet by a friend. The public expectations are different when it comes to the royals, hence the royal standard requires painful discipline. **Remember, you have been adopted and you are now royalty!**

Observe the dress sense of the royals. Despite all the fashion trends and worldly cultures associated with music, there is always a nobly modest and generally acceptable dress sense they adhere to, be it casual or formal. In the casual dressing of a prince, you will not find him wearing his pants hanging low with underpants showing. You will not find him with pierced earrings and body tattoos, with inscribed gold chains of Great Britain affirming his royal identity. Although he may love the hip-hop culture, rock culture and the popular trends of the world, it is however not the royal identity and hence he must discipline himself in adhering to royal standards.

Observe the dressing of a princess, you will never find her wearing provocative clothes, showing off her cleavage, thighs or belly. Her choices of shoes are not clear heels, often associated with the sex industry. She does not wear any other body piercing apart from what is generally acceptable for women in her culture. Her hair is well kept, often without bright coloured dyes (green, red etc.) or anything that may appear unusual to cultural norms. During summer, you will not find her wearing hot pants because she is genuinely hot (from the heat of summer) and needs a bit of breeze or tanning. In any and every weather, her dressing is often contemporary, fashionable but never provocative. Although she may acknowledge possessing a beautiful figure especially in the areas where men may find attractive, her identity as a royal requires modesty and self-respect in public appearance. Does she always prefer to dress this way? I believe not, but her identity as a royal demands the painful discipline of forgoing some certain taste in fashion, in order to uphold the identity of the family. **Remember, you have now been adopted into the Royal Family, and hence you must now pay close attention to the image you portray with respect to what you wear.**

Notice the choice of words used by members of the Royal Family. In public speaking, their words are eloquently spoken and often devoid of any profanity. Does this mean they have no knowledge of such swear words? Or are they not entitled to express their anger and frustration using words that voice out their emotions? I believe they are entitled to this, but their identity does not permit the use of such words, especially in the public domain. **Your identity as a royal demand that you show discipline with your choice of words.**

Observe the general conduct of a royal, even when offended in public they exercise self-control at all times. They do not go about exchanging punches or derogative words with people they are not pleased with. They know when to be silent, when to talk, when to walk away and when to engage with others. Their behaviour and manners are always in check, often leaving the public with little or no reason to question their conduct. **Self-control is a key quality of being a royal, hence you must now exercise self-control at all times.**

Even though the example of being adopted by the Queen of England is merely imaginative, the reality for most of us is that we do not live in Buckingham Palace, but we are adopted children of God. If the earthly royal discipline appears to be painful and demanding, how much more the heavenly royal standard? This is by no means a call to revert to legalistic practices as a mere hypocritical show for observers. It is not a call to mimic the practices of the British Royal Family. It is rather a call to a higher form of discipline that displays the identity of the Heavenly Royal Family.

Discipline in outward appearance

A very popular saying among some believers is, "**The Lord looks at my heart and not at my appearance**". This notion has given rise to all kinds of indecent dressing within the church. In recent years, you may look at some of the churches and see children of the kingdom (princes and princesses) dressed in clothes associated with the gangster hip-hop culture, metallic rock culture, sex culture etc. You can now find young men in saggy pants with their boxer shorts showing, wearing big gold chains, diamond earrings, with tattoos of the cross and other images on their arms and visible parts of their body. You find men and women with several body piercings, often associated with the gothic and contemporary youthful look. On the other hand, when dressing formally to church, some intentionally go over the top with expensive designer suits, 'crocodile' skin shoes, expensive chains, watches and other jewelleries to parade their sense of wealth or social status within the church. Some of the women also wear provocative clothes i.e. really short skirts, tight tops that reveal cleavages etc. Most of the time, the notion behind this excessive look is supposedly meant to depict the freedom believers have in Christ; to show off 'God's blessing' upon one's life, or to express one's individuality and personality. The only issue here is that, the church is a place of fellowship and worship where only God must be the centre of all attention. Although some may claim that they only desire to look good, others often have a different motive in mind. The dominant motive is to make a fashion statement that attracts attention and portrays an identity associated with a social status, worldly culture and lustful beauty (the sexy look). Although our salvation is not determined by the clothes we wear, our understanding of our new identity as adopted children of God gives us a better insight into the importance of the image we portray.

During the earthly ministry of Jesus, the Pharisees and Scribes gave much attention to their outward appearance as opposed to their inward (heart) appearance. They wore long robes and kept a long beard. They were well clothed in accordance to the strict Jewish practices, but they were missing something essential; their hearts were not as pure as the appearance they portrayed. They were giving mixed signals from an appearance that did not match with the condition of their hearts. In rebuking their hypocrisy, Jesus said;

"Woe to you, scribes and Pharisees, hypocrites! For you clean the outside of the cup and the plate, but inside they are full of greed and self-indulgence. You blind Pharisee! First clean the inside of the cup and the plate, that the outside also may be clean. "Woe to you, scribes and Pharisees, hypocrites! For you are like whitewashed tombs, which outwardly appear beautiful, but within are full of dead people's bones and all uncleanness. So you also outwardly appear righteous to others, but within you are full of hypocrisy and lawlessness" (Matthew 23:25-28).

It appears that many of the modern churches are at a place where the Lord may say; *"for you appear to clean the **inside** of the cup and the* *plate, but **outside** shows sexual lust, worldly cultures, pride in possession, arrogance, attention seeking etc."*. Some believers are yet again giving mixed signals of an outward appearance that does not match the inward royal identity.

Consider Jesus' rebuke of the Scribes and Pharisees. If He rebuked them for cleaning the outside of the cup (outward appearance) and not the inside (the condition of the heart); this created the perception that the cup was clean and fit for use, until the dirt inside was exposed. Anyone wanting to use the cup will not reject drinking from it, until they see the state of what is within. This is because we generally assume that if the outward appearance of a cup or glass looks clean, it should reflect the condition within; but for the Scribes and Pharisees that wasn't the case.

In contrast, for some Christians, if we profess that the inside of our cup is clean (The Holy Spirit is within), but the outside of our cup looks smeared (our dress sense and attitude raises questions of our Christian identity), who in their right mind if given the choice would want to drink from such a cup? Even if the inside of our cup is decorated with gold and diamonds, a stained looking cup on the outside would see people reject its use before they see the treasure within. The point is this; yes, the Lord looks at our heart, but man perceives and judges by what he sees, tastes, feels and hears. We do not have the ability to discern the heart of man, but we have been given our senses to help in such discernment to make our own judgements. With regards to this, Jesus said;

"You will recognize them by their fruits. Are grapes gathered from thornbushes, or figs from thistles? So, every healthy tree bears good fruit, but the diseased tree bears bad fruit. A healthy tree cannot bear bad fruit, nor can a diseased tree bear good fruit. Every tree that does not bear good fruit is cut down and thrown into the fire. Thus you will recognize them by their fruits" (Matthew 7:16-20).

Although this statement is related to identifying false prophets and teachers, Jesus emphasized that by their fruits you will know them. Every fruit tree can mainly be identified by the fruit it produces. In the midst of numerous trees, one can spot a specific tree by its fruit. You may not know what an apple tree looks like, but if you see an apple on the tree, you will say it's an apple tree. Using your sense of sight, you can confidently discern the type of tree it is even before you have tasted of its fruit.

On the other hand, if you had a growing apple plant and as it matured it produced lemon fruits, it would take a lot to convince anyone that you had initially planted an apple seed. Hence, the type of seed in the soil must produce of its own fruits, and the type of fruits must be evident of the initial seed sown. If as Christians we believe that the **seed of God** is now in us (1 John 3:9), then the fruits we bear must also be of the nature of that seed (God). The nature and identity of God must therefore grow and infuse every area of our life, changing our very nature into His. If we claim to be children of light, and yet we are clothed with what is associated with a dark culture, how can the world see this light within us? If we say we are Christians, and yet some dress like thugs and prostitutes, who will believe our testimony that Christ saves and transform lives, if by our appearance we still look like we are in sin.

In 2012 to 2013, I worked as a Programmes Coordinator in a humanitarian organisation based in Niger. Niger is located in the Sahel region. According to CIA World Factbook[7], the country is approximately 80% Muslim. Although I worked in a Christian organisation, there was the policy of employing junior staff members of other faiths who respected the Christian ethos of the organisation. As I engaged a Muslim colleague in conversation, she expressed a concerned she found among Christian women. She had heard some of the Gospel from our

---

[7] *The World Factbook, Africa, Niger. Religion. 2014.* Available from (https://www.cia.gov/library/publications/the-world-factbook/geos/ng.html) [2nd March 2015]

daily morning devotion and prayer, but she remained unconvinced for a number of reasons. One of her reason was that, we Christians do not follow the whole teachings and examples of the Bible when it comes to outward appearance. She went on to state that many of the paintings and sculptures of Mary the mother of Jesus depicts her with a covering on her hair and her whole body. In her opinion, this was a clear example for believers to follow, whereas many of the Christian women did otherwise. She told me of how this had affected the work of a missionary team that visited a village from America. The local tradition in Niger is as such that women do not lead religious prayers or teaching in a mixed setting. This meant, the missionary women were only allowed to talk to the women of the village, while the men were separated. My colleague stated that as they gathered, the local women were surprised at the sight of how these missionaries were dressed. She explained, some of the women wore shorts, shirts and sandals, while others wore clothes that were traditionally unacceptable especially within the villages. I can personally understand why the missionary women were dressed that way, since temperatures in the capital of Niger (Niamey) could reach as high as 43 degrees Celsius. Sadly, it was said one of the local women made a startling comment to the group gathered. She said to them, *"How can these women teach us anything about God if they do not know how to dress properly?"* With that said, my colleague narrated that the local women refused to listen to anything the visitors had to say about the Christian faith. It was embarrassing for the missionaries who had claimed to come with Good News from God, but to the locals, it appeared that the good news had not transformed their lives. In this experience, while religious norms and local traditions had a significant role to play in the outcome of events, it however highlights how important a role our outward appearance plays in our daily lives of evangelism.

My personal experience with the image we portray was made apparent to me as I walked home from a prayer meeting one evening. Having been in an uplifting service in the presence of God, I kept the mood of worship through the playlist I had on my phone. Being bald in appearance and walking home on a cold evening of February, I wore a hooded jumper that covered my head. As I made my way from church, I had barely reached 300 meters into my journey when a young man stopped and motioned towards me. I lowered my hood and took out my earphones. His question to me was, **"Mate, do you know anyone who 'shots' (sells weed) around here?"** I responded with a surprise look on my face, as I said NO! He quickly hurried on to avoid any reactions from me since he clearly perceived I deemed his question offensive. Walking on, I pondered on what had happened and I realised that, although I was free to dress as I pleased and had no intentions of portraying any image contrary to my Christian faith; my style of clothing could unfortunately be associated with the contemporary street UK identity. Reflecting on my experience, I doubted the young man would have asked every passer-by the same question he had asked me. He however looked at my appearance and made his judgements accordingly. Out of the few people that passed by him, I appeared as his ideal fit for the link to a local drug dealer (i.e. young man, physically built, wearing a black hooded jumper with hood up to obscure face [*my actual intention was to cover my bald head to keep me warm*], tracksuit bottoms and trainers). I must admit, I looked like one. I can imagine him saying to himself, "*Bingo, that's our guy!*". Contrary to his perception, I am a Christian who is active in preaching the Word of God and seeing lives transformed by the Gospel. What I would have rather expected was for him to enquire about a local church or about my faith in Christ, but the identity I had portrayed in appearance was not one that can often be associated with the church.

As Christians, our freedom in Christ is as such that there is no particular type of dress sense we must adhere to, except for that which is modest and appropriate. A familiar scripture on this topic that has often sparked extreme reactions is 1 Timothy 2:9-10, which states;

"likewise also that women should adorn themselves in respectable apparel, with modesty and self-control, not with braided hair and gold or pearls or costly attire, but with what is proper for women who profess godliness—with good works."

On one extreme, you may have some believers who may read this and perceive it as the absolute godly standard for Christian women. They may even read it literally as meaning; women should not braid their hair, lace it with gold or pearls or wear costly attire because this is ungodly. On the other extreme, some may pretend that such scriptures do not exist, and if they do, they are irrelevant, too legalistic or dated. I believe the best way to view this scripture is to perceive the principle behind it. The Apostle used three key words; respectable, modesty and self-control. Ultimately, these are some precious inward virtues of a Christian's identity, hence the emphasis is to focus on building this, rather than giving a greater attention to the external. In other words, this internal beauty must be an equal representation of the external.

I doubt I would have expressed an interest in my wife if on the first day we met, I saw her in some old clothes looking unkempt. I doubt that this was what the Apostle meant for Christian women, but the principle behind this is to be intentional in using these three virtues as a way of discerning what is appropriate and godly.

A Christian's identity is found in Christ and hidden in God, hence he/she must feel comfortable wearing clothes that are culturally acceptable in the region he/she resides in. The only issue here is, where does one draw a line between what is generally acceptable and unacceptable in a culturally diverse and globalised world? While this question may appear problematic, there is however a cross-cutting acceptable dress sense for men and women in this globalised world, where majority of people from various backgrounds can agree on it suitability.

But in truth, as Christians, though cultural norms may play a role in the type of clothes we wear, our source of approval must not be determined by the trends of the world but rather by the knowledge that springs from our new found identity in Christ. Having this knowledge should guide one to question two main things about their choice of clothing.

a) **Motive**: Is there any motive behind what we have chosen to wear? (i.e. to attract attention by showing off our body, to portray a sense of pride or wealth, to promote a worldly culture we will like to be associated with etc.)
b) **Message**: What message does our dressing convey? What does it say about our faith? What perception does it create? (i.e. modest, sexy, street, neutral, sports etc.)

Despite the fact that the dress sense and appearance of a Christian does not determine if one is saved or not (*unless it is intentionally done to lead others into temptation or sin*), it however speaks of what the heart inclines towards. A heart that loves the hip hop or rock culture will in **most cases** display evidences of such fruits through the style of clothing. A heart that loves to be the centre of attention, often causing heads to turn may do so through what they wear. The one who takes pride in his/her riches may express this through the expensive clothes and matching accessories. Others who delight in their beauty may dress in a way to call attention to their best assets. Sadly, the perception of beauty has gradually evolved as secularism has arisen. The worldly perception of female beauty can now be associated with how many men one can cause to lustfully stare at them. This notion is supposedly meant to help increase a woman's confidence as they feel needed by the opposite sex. In the area of clothing, the quickest option to attain this supposed level of confidence is to make the clothes tighter, shorter and revealing. Unfortunately, this idea has caught on with some believers who through their pursuit of wanting to look their best, have struggled to differentiate between the worldly and the godly.

Ultimately, a heart that is truly transformed by the power of the Gospel and the knowledge of an identity in Christ, will be more inclined to pleasing God through a discipline in outward appearance, since that person understands his/her heavenly royal identity (i.e. I am now a prince or a princess of God, hence I adhere to a heavenly kingdom standard and not the standards of the world).

Discipline in Grace

Through the blood of Christ, God has called us and adopted us into His heavenly royal family. You are of royalty now, spiritually clothed with garments of righteousness, a cape of holiness and surrounded by the purest of light. You are under a new order, governed by heavenly royal principles as detailed in the Bible and taught to you by your private mentor, the Holy Spirit. As children of God, even though all these provisions are made available to us, including being given earthly shepherds i.e. pastors and teachers, we still sometimes find ourselves alternating between the old identity and the new royal identity. Many Christians love the fact that they are children of God through Christ, and while many are happy to welcome the blessings that come with this new found identity, not all are equally enthusiastic about the painful discipline of a royal.

Among many other factors, the rise in the idea of being 'open-minded' as a church has in one way benefited the body of Christ, but to an extent it has also distorted our conception of Christian discipline. A popular saying among some believers is that, "**we are under grace and not under the law**". While this notion is firmly rooted in the Bible as taught by Apostle Paul (Romans 6:14), you may find that some believers misuse this expression as an excuse for indiscipline. Example: Most believers will never miss a day off work except on the grounds of illness or holiday. On the contrary, when it's about the church, some develop a very lax approach to attendance, studying of the word or prayer, using as excuses the grounds of grace. Some also develop a very laidback or passive form of discipline in righteousness, often comfortable to live in the grey areas where sin can be tolerated or entertained once a while. You may find others who may regularly test the waters of sin and then repent, not out of a true conviction of sin but rather as a means of self-comfort or assurance that they are back in God's good books.

In his book, *Generous Justice*, Timothy Keller made a profound statement as he said, *"The classic Christian doctrine is that on the cross Jesus actually saved us by standing in our place and paying our debt to the law of God. If the Lord takes his law so seriously that he could not strug off our disobedience to it, that he had to become human, come to earth, and die a terrible death – then we must take that law very seriously too"*[8].

This statement is by no means suggesting that we return back to basics of adhering the laws of Moses as a way of meriting our righteousness. It is rather pointing us to the place of acknowledging the importance of God's laws, as we make a conscious decision (commitment) to submit to the Lordship of Christ Jesus. Too often, some Christians appear reluctant to empty themselves of the fleeting pleasures of sin, although deep down, the Lord may have placed the will power to resist temptation to that sin. Having a misconception of what grace truly means, some have created for themselves what appears to be a 'perfect solution'; **sin now and repent later**! Others also take on a very vulnerable position, saying things like, "I am only human". This is often said to convey a sympathising notion to a portrayed susceptibility to sin.

But then again, as Christians, we have been called to *"bear with the failings of the weak, and not to please ourselves"* (Romans 15:1). Despite being matured in the faith and highly esteemed among the

---

[8] Keller. T,. 2010. *Generous Justice*. Hodder & Stoughton

early church, Apostle Paul was mindful of the fact that some Christians may take pride in looking down on others who were struggling with the transition from their old identity to the new. He therefore encouraged believers who are 'strong' to bear with the failings of the weak. Bearing with the failings of the weak implies; praying for each other, encouraging each other and teaching one another of how to overcome challenges they face. The act of bearing with the failings of the weak also required a gentle approach to the process of encouragement or teaching. What this does not mean is for Christians to always turn a blind eye to pervading sin, since the act of bearing with one is in hope of becoming better.

Whilst we must build each other up and sympathise with each other's weaknesses as Christ did for us, there comes a time when the Lord may require of us to be disciplined as soldiers, who will stand firm and be clothed with the full armour of God (Ephesians 6:10-18). Among other factors, being fully clothed in that armour requires discipline and maturity in faith. Therefore, as Christians, we must be disciplined enough in righteousness to be able to resist the devil's devices, since indiscipline to some sin may have very severe consequences. It was in reference to this discipline that the writer of the book of Hebrews said;

"And have you forgotten the exhortation that addresses you as sons? "My son, do not regard lightly the discipline of the Lord, nor be weary when reproved by him. For the Lord disciplines the one he loves, and chastises every son whom he receives." It is for discipline that you have to endure. God is treating you as sons. For what son is there whom his father does not discipline? If you are left without discipline, in which all have participated, then you are illegitimate children and not sons. Besides this, we have had earthly fathers who disciplined us and we respected them. Shall we not much more be subject to the Father of spirits and live? For they disciplined us for a short time as it seemed best to them, but he disciplines us for our good, that we may share his holiness" (Hebrews 12:5-10).

The passage is very clear, as adopted children of God we must undergo discipline, since the Lord disciplines every son he receives and loves. Furthermore, it states, "it is for discipline that you have to endure", implying there is a standard of discipline the Lord requires of His children. Therefore, His discipline is meant to build in us the character of Christ the obedient Son. The passage also explains, *"If you are left without discipline, in which all have participated, then you are illegitimate children and not sons"*.

The best explanation to this verse can be compared to the case of Celestine the street kid. Having been abandoned and left on the streets, he lived his own life without any parental guidance to instruct him on what was right or wrong. While on the streets, he begged for food and probably stole from local shops to satisfy his hunger. His manners in relating to adults or even his age mates were mainly guided by his own judgement, hence he may appear to be very rude at times. He had no true sense of the dangers and consequences out there in the world, since no one protected him or taught him how to live in accordance to general principles of life. Unfortunately, due to his mother's death and his father's neglect, Celestine was not considered a son who belonged to a family. **This meant no one took responsibility for his wellbeing, which also included the shaping of his moral character.** But when he was taken in by the church, he was now considered a son and hence had to undergo discipline. There were now rules in place to shape up his character. He was no longer permitted to beg on the streets. He was enrolled in school to develop his manners and literacy level. He was taught to obey adults and refrain from using derogative words. He was now under curfew and had to be back on church premises at a set time. All these measures were put in place for his own good, in shaping a character of self-discipline. Even though he may have found this new change somewhat painful and challenging, he gradually made that transition into his new way of life. Using Celestine's example, the passage therefore simply means, because we are now adopted children of God, our heavenly Father has full responsibility to ensure we are disciplined children belonging to His family. Our obedience and reverence to Biblical teachings are some signs of the discipline we must endure, indicating God's authority as our Father over our lives.

The Loving but firm discipline of the Lord

"For the Lord disciplines the one he loves, and chastises every son whom he receives" (Hebrews 12:6).

The degree of discipline each believer undergoes varies in relation to their level of maturity in faith. Note that in describing this type of discipline, the writer makes a transition between using the word disciplines to chastises. In the King James Version, the words used are more forceful as compared to the ESV, but this gives us a clear picture of the change in the approach of discipline. The King James Version uses the words, **chasteneth** and then **scourgeth**. The word chasten could also mean discipline, correct, subdue or punish, but its focus is more on disciplining through teaching and correcting for moral improvements. On the other hand, the word scourge focuses more on punishment, or corporal punishment as a result of one's continuous disobedience. The modern Christian may find this notion a bit unsettling, since the attributes of God that is often taught in most churches is in reference to His unfailing love, grace and mercy. Furthermore, there is now a growing notion that scourging is not for loved sons but rather for unbelievers. Additionally, the modern society may find the act of disciplining through scourging (i.e. smacking, whipping etc.) a bit primitive or even barbaric. For that reason, why should God scourge those He claims to love? I believe that with reference to how the writer of Hebrews used the word chasten to precede the word scourge, this implies that the Lord only scourges at the last resort. The scourging of the Lord is therefore not His first choice of discipline, but rather His final option that is sure to get us back on track. Our identity as legitimate children of a righteous and impartial God may see us disciplined or even scourged to shape us as Kingdom Citizens.

An example of God's scourging was evident in how He dealt with David, the man He said was after His own heart (1 Samuel 13-14 and Acts 13:22). Many passages in the Old Testament spoke of God's love for David, yet the impartial righteousness of God led to his scourging when he overstepped his boundaries into grievous sin. The Bible states that during his reign, King David had sent his army to war against the Ammonites, while he remained in Jerusalem. When the men were away, the passage says;

"It happened, late one afternoon, when David arose from his couch and was walking on the roof of the king's house, that he saw from the roof a woman bathing; and the woman was very beautiful. And David sent and inquired about the woman. And one said, "Is not this Bathsheba, the daughter of Eliam, the wife of Uriah the Hittite?" So David sent messengers and took her, and she came to him, and he lay with her. (Now she had been purifying herself from her uncleanness.) Then she returned to her house. And the woman conceived, and she sent and told David, "I am pregnant."" (2 Samuel 11:2-5).

This passage is a clear example of the battle between our strong human desires and our obedience to the way of the Lord. It is very obvious that on this occasion, David had made up his mind to pursue what he really wanted even though he was offered several escape routes prior to actually committing sin.

Escape route 1: David had the opportunity to exercise self-control and restraint when he first saw a naked woman bathing. His obedience to the voice of the Holy Spirit should have made him look away, but he kept staring until he acknowledged that she was beautiful. If he but only restrained himself from looking, he would have escaped.

Escape route 2: David went on to enquire about the beautiful woman he saw. This is a clear step of his intension to pursue this woman. If he but only restrained himself from pursuing after looking, he would have escaped.

Escape route 3: After enquiring about the woman, David was told that she was **married** to Uriah the Hittite. This is a big sign board saying, "NO! PROCEED NO FURTHER!" It is at this point that the fear of the Lord and the reverence of His law should have flooded David's heart, leading him to exercise self-control and obedience, nonetheless David proceeded.

Escape route 4: David then sent for the woman to be brought to him. From the time his servants were sent out, till the time the woman arrived were several minutes to an hour (probably more). Consider how long it takes for women to generally get ready for events. Now consider how long it might take for a woman to prepare for a meeting with the king. It is obvious that David had time on his hands to carefully think about his proposed actions prior to Bathsheba's arrival. This was more than enough time to have sent messengers to abort mission, but no, David was determined to have her.

Escape route 5: Upon her arrival, although David had reached the pinnacle of his sexual lust and probably couldn't wait to fulfil his desires, he still had the authority to just entertain her presence without making it a bedroom affair. David was however determined to see it through, hence he gladly yielded his self-control in exchange for fulfilling his sexual pleasures.

Subsequent to gratifying his sexual desires with a married woman, David received a message stating that Bathsheba was pregnant. Knowing that this news will tarnish his royal identity and his moral standing with the law, he sought to resolve it by trickery. Additionally, the consequences of such news may see Bathsheba publicly humiliated, or in an extreme case face the death penalty according to the Law of

Moses (Leviticus 20:10). The king had to act swiftly to avoid any of these outcomes. The passage goes on to explain that David sent a message to summon Uriah (the husband of Bathsheba) from the war front to the palace. When Uriah arrived, David enquired about the situation on the ground. Having appeared satisfied by the news Uriah gave, he proceeded to reward him by sending him home to lay with his wife. This was a move that David had thought would cover up his sin. Unfortunately, Uriah did not go home but slept at the door of the king's house with the other guards. When David heard about this and questioned Uriah's unusual choice of action, he responded by saying;

"The ark and Israel and Judah dwell in booths, and my lord Joab and the servants of my lord are camping in the open field. Shall I then go to my house, to eat and to drink and to lie with my wife? As you live, and as your soul lives, I will not do this thing." (2 Samuel 11:11).

This was a very genuine response from a loyal soldier who can identify with his suffering comrades on the field. His response was also a dagger that pierced the conscience of David, as he now deliberated why he ever did such a thing to a very loyal servant. It is also clear that luring Uriah with the prospect of having passionate sex with a beautiful wife, was not enough to convince him to go home. This was a man of honour who was sure to keep his word. In a desperate attempt to carve out an escape route, David invited him to dinner, where he ate and made him drunk. Excessive alcohol was certain to affect any man's self-control, maybe he will give in to the temptation of going home to his wife. But yet again, Uriah was determined not to go home, as he slept on the couch of the palace with the servants of the king. Having run out of options, the next morning, David took extreme measures that were out of his godly character. He wrote a letter to Joab the commander of his army and sent it by the hand of Uriah. *"In the letter he wrote "Set Uriah in the forefront of the hardest fighting, and then draw back from him, that he may be struck down, and die""*. (2 Samuel 11:15). Joab followed the king's orders and Uriah was killed in battle. The final verse of the passage says, *"... the thing that David had done displeased the LORD"* (2 Samuel 11:27).

Even though David was loved by the Lord and was considered a child of God, his actions were far from the godly kingdom principles he often expressed through deeds, songs and written psalms. David was not a perfect man, hence the grace of God upheld him in his weakness; but on this occasion, David had overstepped the boundaries of sin into the dark dimension of pure evil. His actions were out of character and devoid of anything godly or righteous. David had not only crossed the boundary of sin, but had also passed over from chastisement into scourging. Maybe if he had only committed adultery, he may have been chastised by the Lord. David however took another man's wife, laid with her and tried to use trickery to cover up his sin. When it all failed, he deliberately planned the murder of an innocent man who was very loyal to him. Undoubtedly, the righteous and impartial nature of God meant that David's actions deserved nothing less than the scourging from a loving Father.

The Lord sent Nathan the prophet to pronounce the scourging of David as a result of this sin (See 2 Samuel 12:9-15).

1) He will experience the violent death (the sword) of family members even as he had also order the death of Uriah. This was fulfilled when his son Amnon was killed by his brother Absalom. Furthermore, Absalom was also killed during his rebellion against the rule of David.

2) His wives were to be taken and given to his neighbour, who would lie with them *'in the sight of the sun'*. The Lord said, *"For you [David] did it secretly, but I will do this thing before all Israel and before the sun"* (2 Samuel 12:12). This was fulfilled when David's son Absalom laid with his father's concubines in a tent that was set on the roof top of the palace during his rebellion. (2 Samuel 16:20-22)

3) The son of David that was conceived by Bathsheba through adultery was to die. This was fulfilled when the child fell terribly ill and died as a baby

These harsh consequences give us an insight into the righteousness of God's judgement and His faithfulness to execute justice for all, even at the expense of scourging His beloved children. Then again, the love of God was still apparent throughout David's scourging. While Nathan the prophet was pronouncing these judgements against David, he became alarmed to the reality of his sin as he exclaimed in repentance, *"I have sinned against the LORD"!* Immediately, Nathan replied, *"The LORD also has put away your sin; you shall not die"*. God's unending love was reassuring David that regardless of how painful this scourging might be; He is still his loving Father.

Additionally, even though David lost the child that Bathsheba bore for him, the Lord gave them another son called Solomon. Solomon was also to be named Jedidiah (meaning, *beloved of the Lord*), this was a reassuring message of God's unchanging love for David, as he sent good news of the child's name by Nathan the prophet. Moreover, despite the severe scourging David underwent because of his sin, Solomon his son was exceedingly blessed by the Lord as he became the next king of Israel. Solomon was also truly beloved of the Lord, being blessed with great wisdom and understanding which led to his prominence throughout the whole ancient world. Furthermore, Israel as a nation prospered greatly under his rule, enjoying peace and security during his reign.

As adopted children of God through Christ, it is always comforting to know that we are beloved of the Lord always. In the midst of chastening or scourging, may we respond in humble repentance, knowing that the firm hand of the Lord is also tender and soothing to heal. In acknowledging this truth, Eliphaz the friend of Job said, *"Behold, blessed is the one whom God reproves; therefore despise not the discipline of the Almighty. For he wounds, but he binds up; he shatters, but his hands heal"* (Job 5:17-18).

Ultimately, the whole point of undergoing any form of discipline as children of God, be it chastening or scourging, is to produce a character of obedience in adhering to a moral standard that forms a part of our new identity. As children adopted into the kingdom of God, the discipline of the Lord is evident of two main things.

1) It speaks of our identity as sons belonging to the family of God, with moral principles and standards we must adhere to.

2) It shows that God has not abandoned us to our own ways, but rather He still takes a keen interest in our spiritual welfare and maturity in Christ Jesus.

We may undergo discipline in certain seasons of our lives, but our Lord is also quick to reward our obedience through blessings unimaginable.

Heavenly Sons, Earthly Experiences

HEAVENLY SONS, EARTHLY EXPERIENCES

All the promises in the Bible concerning one's identity in Christ are true and are made available to us by faith. However, some readers may question why they may not have experienced some of the richness of this reality in their lives. Perhaps you have been a Christian for years and yet you still struggle with low self-esteem or sense of worth. It seems your Christian identity has not changed much of this feeling. Maybe you are a Christian who desires more of the spiritual experience of your faith but everything seems so natural. Why is that?

We cannot answer all these questions, but below are five basic points that should take us a step closer in exploring this new identity we have in Christ.

1. Seasons of life
2. More knowledge and understanding of one's new identity
3. Improved prayer life and fellowship with God
4. More daring faith
5. Maturing as a believer

Seasons of life

As adopted children of God who are still in this world, we have a limited experience of the full riches of God until His appointed time when we will be with Him. What we currently have is a foretaste of the fullness that is to come, but this is still more than sufficient for us

The Bible details amazing stories of God's great provision for His people. In the Old Testament, we see a recurring correlation between obedience and success, or obedience and favour. If you want to live in abundance of blessings, obey God and be good. However, we also find that some of the shabbiest dressed people were good men of God (prophets) who had a really hard time during their ministry. This puts this idea to question, not to doubt its truth, but rather to be careful not to generalise this notion.

As Christians, we may feel very privileged by God's favour and the experience of His love in our lives. We may consider the abundance and security we enjoy in the West, and may somehow think that we have an entitlement to a good stress free life as children of God.

I have even heard some pastors pray for some people by and saying, *"You will never struggle in your life"*. And the person being prayed for replies, *"AMEN!"*.

"You will never suffer in your life".

"AMEN!".

"You will not have a want in your life".

"AMEN!"

After hearing this, I thought to myself, really? The truth is, there is a sense that God forms a hedge around us to protect our lives and our property. He also goes before us to grant us favour with people and in our endeavours. But the idea that we will not face struggles or suffering is exaggerated. You will not find this anywhere in scripture, partly because life is full of seasons and God moves in seasons. Even Jesus and the Apostles experienced a time of hunger and a time of plenty, so what makes us think we are exempted from this?

The gospel according to Mark states that; *"On the following day, when they came from Bethany,* **he [Jesus Christ] was hungry**. *And seeing in the distance a fig tree in leaf, he went to see if he could find anything on* it. *When he came to it, he found nothing but leaves, for it was not the season for figs"* (Mark 11:12-13).

This passage is a clear indication of some of the experiences we may go through in some seasons of life. Even Jesus our Lord in his glory and might, who was able to work miracles to feed thousands of people still experienced a time of hunger and lack. I can imagine His stomach rumbling and being tempted to use His power to call down a great feast from Heaven. Although He had the power to do this, He chose to endure the season. This means, there are some certain things that life throws at us, that we cannot escape but only endure until the season passes.

Reflecting on Jesus' experience, a question to ask is: Did His experience of hunger and suffering nullify His identity as the Son of God? No, it didn't! Because life's seasons of challenges and suffering does not determine our true identity. We are still children of God, irrespective of abundance or lack, good health or ill health, in peace or in persecution.

Acts 11:27-30, details a prophecy concerning a severe famine that was to occur in Judea and around the world during the times of the early church. The passage says, *"Now in these days prophets came down from Jerusalem to Antioch. And one of them named Agabus stood up and foretold by the Spirit that there would be a great famine over all the world (this took place in the days of Claudius). So the disciples determined, every one according to his ability, to send relief to the brothers living in Judea. And they did so, sending it to the elders by the hand of Barnabas and Saul"*.

It is important to note that this famine occurred in Judea and the surrounding regions after the resurrection of Christ and the Baptism of the Holy Spirit. The Christians referred to us brothers, were mostly Spirit filled believers who had experienced miracles being done by the Apostles. Despite the miracles and the evidential power of the Holy Spirit among them, these Christians still had to endure a season of famine. Even more challenging to understand, is the fact that it was God who permitted it and revealed it through Agabus.

For many of us in the West, the idea of famine seems to be a forgotten woe. It is thought of as something of the past that still happens in other poor countries but not in the developed world. I had never experienced famine until I got a job in Niger in 2012. For the first time in my life, I had a brief encounter with its effects and it was not pleasant. The season was characterised by low crop yields, often caused by drought and locust infection. Famine dramatically decreases household consumption, with families eating small rations of food on average one to two meals (if lucky) a day. Famine does not only affect food scarcity, it also affects household income for farmers and traders of agricultural products. If you have no crops, you have nothing to sell on the market. Furthermore, food prices are high during these seasons, with shortages of food supply and its high demands. It is in these times that households adopt coping strategies through sale of their assets (mostly livestock) to ensure their survival. Besides, it's not like they have a choice, because their livestock may die either way for lack of fodder to feed them. Famine does not only rob the affected people of a dignified life today, it also affects their ability to break out of its hold for future progress. This happens when crop yields are so low that households do not get enough seeds from their produce to plant for the next season. Without seeds, you have no hope for food in the next harvest.

It is in response to such disaster that Paul and Barnabas were entrusted with the responsibility of sending relief to the church. Were the Spirit filled Christians exempted from experiencing the seasons of famine and lack, despite the authority and power they had in their new identity? No! If it were so, they would have no need of relief from Paul and Barnabas. But the reality is that, these believers went through the natural seasons of life, scraping every little they could live off and supplementing what they had with the little relief they received. Did this experience make them any less of children of God in comparison to their brothers at Antioch and other regions? No! The harsh experiences of life with its effects does not imply that one is not favoured by God or walking in their Christian identity.

In Apostle Paul's writing to the church of Philippi, he gave the readers an insight into how he has learnt to patiently endure some of these seasons of life. In Philippians 4:11-13, he said; *"Not that I am speaking of being in need, for I have learned in whatever situation I am to be content. I know how to be brought low, and I know how to abound.* ***In any and every circumstance, I have learned the secret of facing plenty and hunger, abundance and need****. I can do all things through him who strengthens me".*

From earlier references, you may note that most of these scriptures that speak of one's identity in Christ were written by Apostle Paul. How then is it that the Apostle appears to claim he experiences a time of need (lack), when he has written much about God's promises in Christ? Once again, the seasons of life are not indicators of one's identity in Christ Jesus. If it were so, then many believers going through challenging times are not in Christ then. The fact that your fellow brother or sister in the faith may presently be experiencing a season of abundance and open doors, does not imply that they are more of a son of the kingdom than you are. You are equally loved by God. You are only going through life's seasons, but as sons of the kingdom, we have a promise from God stating; *"And we know that for those who love God all things work together for good, for those who are called according to his purpose"* (Romans 8:28).

In your season of abundance, praise God for it. Be eager to share your joy with others, as well as being ready to put your arms around those suffering or going through a season of drought. Seasons are never permanent, they eventually change.

More knowledge and understanding of one's new identity

Knowledge and understanding can often be used interchangeably. I however believe that knowledge is the gateway to understanding. Understanding is a deeper and intimate form of knowledge. One may say, "*I know my wife*", and another may say, "*I understand my wife*". Which of these two statements carry a deeper form of familiarity? I believe majority will choose the second, even though both may carry a similar notion. Regarding this, one can claim that without knowing your wife, you cannot understand her. Similarly, without knowing your Bible, you cannot understand or even begin to comprehend your identity in Christ.

Many believers solely rely on the teachings of a Pastor once every week. Many Bibles are abandoned on shelves, taking up dust and being opened on special occasions such as Christmas, Easter etc. How can one gain knowledge without studying? If in the world one must spend approximately twenty-five plus years of their life studying to become a doctor, how then could some believers expect to walk victoriously in an identity they have no clear knowledge of? More so, an identity they do not spend time reading about.

This can be compared to an immigrant that arrived in a new country. Upon arrival, he was given a book that detailed all his entitlement as a foreigner. In reading and understanding what has been written, he can enjoy all the privileges offered to him in that country. His ignorance of his rights and entitlements could make him vulnerable of being taken advantage of. Rather than reading and understanding his entitlements in that nation, he went about living a life far lower than what was promised to him because of his ignorance.

The knowledge of God's word has the power to transform lives. The Bible provides believers with such knowledge and truth of who they are in Christ. The ignorance of one's royal linage could determine if they live as a prince or a pauper. This statement is not to insinuate that knowing the Bible and one's identity in Christ guarantees earthly riches, making one live as an earthly prince/princess. It rather portrays the holistic wellbeing of believers who understand the treasures and riches of knowing Christ and their identity in Him. It is to illustrate ones understanding of God's love for them, the authority in which they walk in, and the glory that is made manifested to them (and also within them) and awaiting them at the coming of Christ.

It is therefore good to sense God's presence and power with chosen men and women of God, but it is however better to know the Word of God for yourself and to walk in your new identity in Christ.

Improved prayer life and fellowship with God

Prayer in its simplest term is our means of communicating with God. Similar to every healthy relationship, a key area of strength is evident of good communication. Having attended many weddings, a frequent piece of advice from experienced married couples to the newlyweds is always to ensure good communication between husband and wife. The importance of good communication reaches far beyond our personal relationship with our spouse or siblings, as it is also the key to successful businesses.

Communication keeps one in tune with the other. It brings both parties to a place of dialogue, where both are shaped by each other's views and opinions. Frequent communication develops mutual understanding and familiarity between both parties, as information is interchanged. Although good communication is practiced by many, prayer is however an area where majority of Christians must give much attention to. The pinnacle of this issue is evident by the proportion of people that attend prayer meetings in comparison to other church services. It is one of the practices that is sometimes misperceived as being for a selected few (elders and ministers) in the church, rather than the whole body of Christ. In other cases, the importance of prayer has been reduced to the means by which believers present their requests to God to satisfy their worldly needs.

Think about what an ideal healthy relationship between parents and children should look like. Now imagine waking up in the morning and seeing your children walking about without acknowledging your presence in the house. Imagine being eager to spend time with them, but none seem interested or ready to even engage in a conversation. Imagine having such a relationship every day, yet the only time your children are close to you or desire to talk with you, is when they are in need or are faced with troubles. Conversely, imagine how fulfilling their life will be, if only they were equally eager to spend time with you. You can provide them with the advice needed to steer them away from coming trouble. They can learn about your life experiences and how you overcame similar difficulties. Through such relationship, they can constantly feel appreciated and motivated by a father or a mother who loves them regardless of what life throws at them.

Similarly, a quality time of prayer brings us into the presence of God, where we are shaped and transformed more into the nature of Christ. It is in prayer and worship that burdens are lifted, faith is restored and power is transferred to enable one walk in their new identity. According to scripture, prior to the day of Pentecost following the ascension of Christ, the disciples were gathered in the upper room where they devoted themselves to prayer (Acts 1:12-14). It was during these days of prayer and worshipping, that they were filled with the Holy Spirit on the day of Pentecost. It was in continuous prayer and being in the presence of God that they were able to exercise their divine authority in healing the sick, casting out demons (etc.) by the power of the Holy Spirit and in the name of Jesus.

The Word of God gives knowledge of one's identity in Christ. Prayer brings one into the presence of God, where there is an impartation and an opportunity to partake of the divine nature. It is in prayer that spiritual warfare is waged. It is through prayer that victories are won, which is evident of one's identity as being more than a conqueror. In prayer, the doors of divine possibilities are laid opened for sons of the kingdom who will only but believe God for the power to do great things for His Kingdom.

May our hearts be opened to perceive prayer as an opportunity to meet with God and to be transformed by Him, rather than as a means of satisfying our worldly needs.

More daring faith

Walking in your new identity requires faith, considering that the basis of Christianity is founded on faith in Jesus Christ our Lord. It is by the grace of God through faith in Christ that we are saved. It is by having faith in His atoning work on the Cross that we have attained forgiveness of sin and reconciliation with God. It is through faith that we have been joined with Christ and adopted as sons, having been given the Holy Spirit as a guarantee and a seal of our inheritance. Although it is all through faith that we claim to have attained these, it is not a delusion or a fantasy, since by this same faith our lives have been transformed as a testimony of the Gospel.

The writer of the book of Hebrews states that; *"Now faith is the assurance of things hoped for, the conviction of things not seen"* (Hebrews 11:1). In the context of this passage, the word **assurance** carries a notion of certainty, confidence and guarantee; implying that though faith is often related to things presently not seen, it also possesses a dimension of certainty and an inner conviction of its reality.

Faith has always played an integral part of my Christian life, and there are moments when I can particularly relate to the reality of faith having a dimension of certainty, although not seen. In the course of my life, I have been in situations where I have earnestly prayed concerning a matter and subsequently felt an inner peace and assurance that the matter has been dealt with, even though in reality it still prevails. It is with this inner certainty and peace that surpasses the notion of likelihood or wishful thinking, that the reality of the assurance of faith is made manifested. When one stands in this place of faith, doubts and fear are eroded, leaving one fully certain of attaining what they hoped for. It is in this place of faith that one can confidently claim victory, breakthrough and healing, whilst in the physical realm the symptoms may still exist, but only for a little while. This is the assurance that true faith produces.

Contrary to this notion of faith, many believers have misperceived faith as a game of chance, even doubting the certainty of their salvation. If one is unsure that they are truly saved, how can they then walk in an identity that is only evident in individuals that are saved? If the foundation of your faith is based on doubts and insecurity, being unsure of belonging to the Kingdom or not, how can you then exercise your authority and power as an adopted son when in reality you actually believe you are still an orphan (spiritually speaking)?

In observing the experience of the orphaned street kids in Nairobi, Kenya, I noticed that their begging from passer-by's was without much confidence of receiving anything. Every passer-by was a gamble and a chance for the next shilling, but not certainty. If the passer-by was in a good mood and desired to give, it was their happy day! If not, they weren't that disappointed because they did not expect anything anyway. Their action of begging was based on chance and not of faith. On the other hand, being raised in a family with a father and mother; I asked my father for school fees, pocket money and food, not based on chance but rather in faith that he will provide. There were however some requests I made that I knew I was not guaranteed to receive, considering the effects it may have on me. There were other requests I would not dare to make, since I knew it was ultimately not for my good.

Example: Why should I bother asking my dad for a motorbike at the age of twelve? I was too young to have developed good road awareness, therefore I would have placed my life and the life of others at risk. With such a request, I knew that all the faith I had in my dad will never convince him to buy a motorbike for me. Did this change the faith I had in him? No! Did I think he was unable to buy me a motorbike? No! I had all the faith that he could, but I knew it was not for my good. Growing up as a child, I did not receive everything I asked for, but I never once asked in doubt when I knew it was in accordance to my father's will, which was ultimately for my good.

In James 1:6-8, the writer explains the importance of asking in faith as children of God. In explaining this, he said; *"But let him **[the believer]** ask in faith, with no doubting, for the one who doubts is like a wave of the sea that is driven and tossed by the wind. For that person must not suppose that he will receive anything from the Lord; he is a double-minded man, unstable in all his ways"*.

Similar to the faith one would have in a loving parent, God has called us to have faith in Him. Without faith, one is subject under the realm of chance and uncertainty, similar to the example of the street kids begging from passers-by. Their request is based on chance and uncertainty to receive what they ask for. With faith, one operates in the realm of a son, asking in confidence and knowing that he/she will receive in accordance to the will of God.

The idea of asking in accordance to God's will may lead some to perceive the probability of their prayers being answered as mere chance. If God wills, it will happen! If He doesn't, it will not! Although this is true, faith goes further in believing that God will answer our prayers knowing that

He is our loving Father. This confidence we have is similar to asking our earthly parents for food or new clothes. One will never ask from the perspective that if mum or dad wills, I will have some food to eat today. As a child, you are so confident in the ability of your parents to provide for your needs. In most cases, it may even appear absurd to ask for such things, since these are necessities and must be available. This is the faith of a child that belongs to a good earthly family. This must also be the faith of a Christian, because you belong to the family of God.

There are however some requests that as a firm believer, irrespective of the faith we have in God, He will never answer such prayers. **Example**: Some years ago, I over head a conversation where a gentleman was saying to his friend, "*I am praying that this card deal (credit card fraud) goes through*". How could one expect God to answer a prayer that would defraud others and cause them financial struggles and distress? Even if one has faith as big as a mountain, as opposed to having faith as small as a mustard seed, God will not answer such a prayer.

A similar prayer that many may have prayed in vain is to win the Lottery! Yes, we can all do much good with all that money, but could it ultimately steer us away from God? Could it have an effect on our Christian life and morals? I believe that as a loving Father God is, He knows that the pleasures and temptations that comes with over-night riches could lead one in a path contrary to the way of truth and righteousness. Therefore, for the many lottery players and gamblers, it is truly a game of chance and not of faith.

God is however calling believers to come to a better understanding of their identity in Christ, where their faith in God is firmly grounded and far surpassing any odds of winning from a game of chance. This is a place of faith where you know that you can rest in God, despite the storms and challenges of life. This is a place of a son (a child of God), who is always confident that Father is in control.

On the other hand, you may find some believers operating solely in the realm of faith, when in reality that faith calls for actions to be taken in producing results. Having experienced some past seasons of unemployment, I can confidently say that in **most** (not all) cases, there is no amount of faith one can place in God that will guarantee you a job **without first taking the necessary steps to apply for that job**. The responsibility on your part is not only to have faith, but also to take the necessary steps in improving your CV and actually applying for the job. Another example is: you may attend some Christian events where the organisers have prayed fervently for the success of the programme, yet the actual programme wasn't as successful as anticipated. In some cases, the responsibility of effective planning and organising was not given much attention to ensure the success needed. Therefore, faith can never be a substitute for a lack of planning, training, studying and executing one's responsibility. It is in explaining this that the writer in James said; *"For as the body apart from the spirit is dead, so also faith apart from works is dead"* (James 2:26). In many ways, our faith is not independent from our works (responsibility and actions), but rather both work in conformity and interdependently for the desired outcome.

Blind Bartimaeus knew his responsibility and the part he had to play in receiving his healing, when he shouted; *"Jesus, Son of David, have mercy on me!"* (Mark 10:47-48). After being called by the Lord and asked what he wanted done for him, he replied, *"Rabbi, let me recover my sight"* (Mark 10:51).

The paralytic man who was bedridden and brought to Jesus via the roof top did not only have faith, but knew the part he had to play by perhaps convincing his family or friends to carry him to the Lord. He understood and obeyed the Lord's word, when told to, *"...rise, pick up your bed, and go home"* (Mark 2:3-12). He did exactly that and received his full healing. His faith was in conformity with the actions he took.

The woman with the issue of blood, having spent all her money on medications and was still unwell, knew that Christ Jesus was her answer. Her faith in the Son of God quickened her in seizing the opportunity to grab hold of that which will make her well by faith (Luke 8:43-48). Her faith was expressed as she walked towards the Lord and grabbed the fringe of His garment. She knew the part to play in receiving her healing by faith. This is not implying that her action was what made her well, but rather the faith that led her actions. This story also takes us into a deeper understanding of the power and authority of faith. The passage explains that the woman *"came up behind him [Jesus] and touched the fringe of his garment, and immediately her discharge of blood ceased"* (Luke 8:44). The highlight of the passage is not really about her healing, but rather the **unauthorized dispatch of power that was taken by faith**. The passage goes on to state, *"And Jesus said, "Who was it that touched me?" When all denied it, Peter said, "Master, the crowds surround you and are pressing in on you!"* **But Jesus said, "Someone touched me, for I perceive that power has gone out from me"** (Luke 8:45-46). I can picture the scene as the Lord looked almost shocked by the fact that power was dispatched from Him without His consent. I can imagine Him looking at the crowd and saying to Himself; *"Who dares to take power from the King of kings and Lord of lords?" "Who else could have this authority on earth?"* This poor woman had no power in herself, but it was her faith in the Lord that claimed her healing. God had already approved her healing when she first believed, but this reality was made evident in the dispatch of power as she touched the Lord's garment.

Faith is hence an important part of our new identity in Christ; for in faith, everything promised in the Word of God is made available and active. As detailed in some of the examples given in the passages, believers must also act in line with their faith to receive God's promises and blessings.

There are a few cases where it appears a believer has faith and may have done what is required of that faith, but in reality they are lacking in true faith. Such was the case of the man who brought his son suffering from epilepsy to the Lord. In the book of Mark 9:14-27, the story was narrated as follows;

*"And when they came to the disciples, they saw a great crowd around them, and scribes arguing with them. And immediately all the crowd, when they saw him, were greatly amazed and ran up to him and greeted him. And he asked them, "What are you arguing about with them?" And someone from the crowd answered him, "Teacher, I brought my son to you, for he has a spirit that makes him mute. And whenever it seizes him, it throws him down, and he foams and grinds his teeth and becomes rigid. So I asked your disciples to cast it out, and they were not able." And he answered them, "O faithless generation, how long am I to be with you? How long am I to bear with you? Bring him to me." And they brought the boy to him. And when the spirit saw him, immediately it convulsed the boy, and he fell on the ground and rolled about, foaming at the mouth. And Jesus asked his father, "How long has this been happening to him?" And he said, "From childhood. And it has often cast him into fire and into water, to destroy him. **But if you can do anything**, have compassion on us and help us." And Jesus said to him, "**'If you can'! All things are possible for one who believes**." Immediately the father of the child cried out and said, "**I believe; help my unbelief**!" And when Jesus saw that a crowd came running together, he rebuked the unclean spirit, saying to it, "You mute and deaf spirit, I command you, come out of him and never enter him again." And after crying out and convulsing him terribly, it came out, and the boy was like a corpse, so that most of them said, "He is dead." But Jesus took him by the hand and lifted him up, and he arose."*

This particular case is a clear indication that, while some believers may take the necessary steps which could appear to be an act of faith, their actual belief of receiving that which they desire could be in doubt. The man in the story brought his son to the Lord for a healing which he did not entirely believe the Lord could do. This was evident in his statement when he said; *"But if you can do anything, have compassion on us and help us"*. His choice of word, **"IF"**, carries a notion of uncertainty and doubt. Maybe you can do it Lord, maybe you cannot! In response to this, the Lord said; *"If you can'! All things are possible for one who believes"*.

Faith is therefore more than just doing what is required of you and **hoping** for the best. It is rather, you doing your best and knowing that your loving Father has approved of it and has already given that which you need. This view of faith does not imply that as believers, we may never have to wait on the Lord anymore. It is rather a motivation to know that our waiting is not in vain, because He whom we call our Father is an all able God.

Abraham had to endure the process of patiently and even painfully waiting on the Lord for decades before the promise of a son became a reality. Sometimes, we have to undergo the prolonged periods of waiting in faith, not exactly knowing when the Lord will bring our request into reality. The seasons of waiting are uncomfortable and uneasy to bear, especially when one feels they need a desperate intervention. Abraham must have felt this way when Sarah his wife was approaching her menopause years. He probably felt that it was now or never Lord! Those years came and went, yet there was no sign of a child. Even Sarah felt it was a hopeless attempt to have such faith, when it became obvious that the physical possibility of it happening was next to nothing. This was evident in her action of convincing Abraham to take Hagar her servant as a wife, who bore him a son (Genesis 16:1-4). The promise of a child however came to pass several years later, after Sarah's menopause had taken full effect (at ninety years old), after Abraham's body had exceedingly aged (hundred years old), after his faith had undergone severe fatigue from the years of holding on to

God's promise. In spite of this, the promise became a reality as Abraham and Sarah engaged in the probably awkward process of sexual intercourse (considering their advanced age), in faith of receiving a son. Even in their advanced age, they still had to play their part in making the promise a reality after years of waiting.

Ultimately, experiencing the power of God and the authority in our new found identity calls for a bold faith. This is the faith that springs from the knowledge of truth that you are now a child of God (Romans 8:16) and a fellow heir with Christ (Romans 8:17). Being a child of God means, we now have a spiritual heavenly royal linage. Our asking should therefore be in faith and boldness, knowing that it is done by our loving Father. This type of faith also stems from the understanding that *"he [Christ Jesus] who is in you is greater than He who is in the world"* (1 John 4:4). Other similar scriptural truths state; *"I have been crucified with Christ. **It is no longer I who live, but Christ who lives in me.** And the life I now live in the flesh I live by faith in the Son of God, who loved me and gave himself for me"* (Galatians 2:20).

The message in these passages are irrefutably claiming that, although we live in this body, the reality of our spiritual identity is Christ living in us by the power of the Holy Spirit. Our understanding of this opens the doors to the realm of many possibilities, since our laying on of hands, rebuking of demons, prayer, speaking life into dead situations etc. is not only done by us, but by the Spirit of Christ who lives in us. When we declare a thing, we declare it in boldness and in faith, knowing that Christ in us has also declared it.

We are also encouraged by the power of the name of Jesus, when He said, *"All authority in heaven and on earth has been given to me"* (Matthew 28:18). Again He said, *"Whatever you ask in my name, this I will do, that the Father may be glorified in the Son. If you ask me anything in my name, I will do it"* (John 14:13-14). In prayer, our faith and confidence therefore rests in the authority and power of His name. When we declare the name of Jesus in faith and in the understanding of its power, our prayers are no longer just a formality of hope, but rather a declaration in authority (not in one's authority but rather in Christ) and power to bring everything to subjection of that name. Have faith in God and in the power of the name of Jesus Christ!

Maturing as a believer

In the book of Galatians 4:1-2, Apostle Paul made a profound statement when he said; *"I mean that the heir, as long as he is a child, is no different from a slave, though he is the owner of everything, but he is under guardians and managers until the date set by his father"*. The context of this passage is in continuation of Apostle Paul's teaching on the significance of faith as compared to the law. While the passage is an analogy of how in the fullness of time the grace of God through faith has given us all things as heirs in Christ, it also points to the fact that in its literal sense, maturing as a believer is essential.

Having been adopted into the family of God, being justified by grace through faith in the atoning work of the Cross, we are now heirs of the Kingdom. Yet, the passage still states; *"the heir, as long as he is a child, is no different from a slave, though he is the owner of everything, but he is under guardians and managers until the date set by his father"*. This statement can give us a glimpse into the affairs of a royal family.

The innocence of a child is as such that, though they may be royalty, their immaturity and understanding to fully comprehend their identity, authority, **responsibility**, wealth etc. leaves them in the shadow of their teachers and guardians until they reach maturity. Apostle Paul compares this experience to that of a slave. This does not imply that a prince or princess is subject to labour without pay, rather it looks at how a slave is often led by his/her master's commands in the same way that a young prince or a princess is led by their personal teacher, advisor or manager. Without such guidance or mentoring to maturity, a royal child will be ill-prepared to effectively execute their role as a future king.

To give an example: What good is it to give a child of about the age of ten years old a thousand pounds in cash from their inheritance, even if their full inheritance is worth £1,000,000. Firstly, being a child, they cannot comprehend the true value of that money. They might lose it and not even think of its implications. They might misuse it on unnecessary things to please their childhood pleasures without giving much consideration to the future. To fully grasp the implication of such a decision, the Lord explains it better in the story of the prodigal son (Luke 15:11-32), who being the youngest son demanded his inheritance and then squandered it. In real life, any parent or guardian will also be reluctant to give away inheritance to an immature or ill-prepared child. Now consider this; if our earthly parents perceive the idea of maturity in age, conduct and understanding as the best indicators to determine the proper time of giving inheritance, how much more the things of God?

In Apostle Paul's letter to Timothy, he gives us a glimpse into the standard of maturity in spiritual conduct that a pastor/church overseer should possess. In 1 Timothy 3:1-7 he said;

"The saying is trustworthy: If anyone aspires to the office of overseer, he desires a noble task. Therefore an overseer must be above reproach, the husband of one wife, sober-minded, self-controlled, respectable, hospitable, able to teach, not a drunkard, not violent but gentle, not quarrelsome, not a lover of money. He must manage his own household well, with all dignity keeping his children submissive, for if someone does not know how to manage his own household, how will he care for God's church? He must not be a recent convert, or he may become puffed up with conceit and fall into the condemnation of the devil. Moreover, he

must be well thought of by outsiders, so that he may not fall into disgrace, into a snare of the devil".

Note that in the passage, Apostle Paul made mention that if the believer is a new convert (spiritually immature), such responsibility could lead them in the path of conceit, pride or arrogance (puffed up) and even into the condemnation of the devil. This passage may suggest that spiritual immaturity leaves one vulnerable and ill-prepared to effectively deal with the pressures and challenges of overseeing a church. Immaturity could be displayed in many ways, as evident in one's conduct. Most new converts struggle with the transition process into their new identity in Christ. If they are made a church elder at the early stages of the transition process, they may find it challenging to deal with both the physical and spiritual demands of ministry.

In light of this, we can say we have many immature Christians who like the prodigal son, may have hastened to receive the share of their inheritance, thereby taking full responsibility and liability for a gift and a calling they are ill-prepared to execute. You will find that we have some Pastors and Elders who are still immature in the area of self-control, being lovers of money, prideful of worldly possession and weak to sexual lust etc. These immature leaders exploit the ignorance of spiritually immature believers, creating a perception of Christianity that is based on their immature view and understanding of the faith. As a result of this, we frequently hear of disturbing news such as 'a pastor' convincing his church members to eat grass for spiritual growth! WHAT!!? In other churches, you hear of rumours that the church pastor is sleeping with other women within the congregation other than his wife. A more rampant issue is the disguised celebration of greed, pride in possession, and love of money, which has been called the prosperity gospel. Many new believers and unbelievers may find their way into this **"den of robbers"** (Matthew 21:13), hoping to encounter God and the power of His might. Their expectation of a church is left shattered, as they meet a god who will not answer their prayer until they give an offering. In some churches, they are presented with a god who will only give them that child they have longed for many years, after they have paid the 'pastor' some sum of money. In other churches, they are met by a 'pastor' who looks like a male model from a fashion magazine, i.e. curly hair, pierce ears with diamond rings, gold chain with matching watch, designer clothes from head to toe and the latest flashy car. For some of the sheep under his care, it creates a perception of a god who will make you wealthy and exceedingly rich in worldly possession as a Christian. In other churches, this lifestyle is perceived as a right for all Christians, where the pastor takes scriptures out of context to indirectly justify the love of money and the worldly perception of success. If this notion was entirely true, then Christians will be the wealthiest (materially speaking) people on the planet. But the reality is, we have many hardworking Atheist, Muslims, Hindus and believers of other faiths who are billionaires and millionaires as compared to Christians. A visit to India, China, Dubai and other Arab countries will blow this notion (of a Christian God who will make you exceedingly rich) out of water. If one's idea of the Christian God is dependent on the monetary wealth or riches he may get, then I believe one has a better chance in another faith, since the evidence is clear in some Arab and largely unbelieving countries.

Fundamentally, this doctrine is an inaccurate view of the Christian faith being propagated by some Christian leaders who are struggling with all kinds of self-control issues such as greed, love of money and lust. Unfortunately, they either create a culture of believers who follow in these same steps or of unbelievers who think the church is a sham.

Some believers may contend this by saying that a few of the great Men of God in the Bible were wealthy and rich. Some may call the likes of Abraham, Joseph, David, Daniel, and Job as examples of such blessings without fully assessing the spiritual maturity of these men.

Abraham's faith was tried and tested, as evident in his willingness to sacrifice the blessing (Isaac) he received after decades of patiently waiting and trusting God.

Joseph was sold into slavery by his brothers. Just when he thought he had gained some sense of freedom, he was accused of rape and imprisoned again. He spent several years in prison, not losing hope and trusting in God even whiles in the pit. He then became an equivalent of a modern day 'Prime Minister' in Egypt, after being a slave for many years.

David was seen as the least in his family, a shepherd boy who spent years running for his life for fear King Saul would kill him. He was forced to live in the wilderness and in hostile environments, where he was in constant danger. David was even driven to act as though he was insane, dreading his enemies will kill him. Even though he was a king, he was willing to lay aside his royal robes and dignity when it came to worshipping and seeking God.

Can we claim to be as humble as David, as faithful and obedient as Abraham, as persistent in seeking God as Daniel, and as patient and longsuffering as Job and Joseph? These are Men of God who have been tried, tested and proven to be mature and trust worthy in managing the blessings and wealth given by God. These are Men of God who will wilfully lay it all down and be stripped off every wealth only to have God in return. If we are to associate ourselves to the material blessings of these great Men of God, we must equally identify ourselves with their suffering, struggles, challenges and spiritual maturity.

Having considered these, will the Lord trust the gift of working miracles to an immature believer who is still struggling with the issue of greed, pride in possession and love of money? This gift may only lead them in a path where the devil can exploit this weakness, causing them to sin.

Above all, they may propagate an image that is contrary to the true Christian identity, causing many to stumble.

An example of such a case was noted in the book of Acts, when a man named Simon, a local magician, came to faith in Christ (Acts 8:9-11). The passage explains; *"But there was a man named Simon, who had previously practiced magic in the city and amazed the people of Samaria, **saying that he himself was somebody great**. They all paid attention to him, from the least to the greatest, saying, "**This man is the power of God that is called Great.**" And they paid attention to him because for a long time he had amazed them with his magic"*.

From the first few verses, the writer builds a character profile of who this Simon the former magician is. The fact that this man often went about "saying that he himself was somebody great", was evident of a character of pride, arrogance and self-elevation. Furthermore, through his magic, he had built his fame and reputation as the man who embodied the power of God called Great. Simon was obviously a local celebrity who was well known by all, and possibly idolised for his magical powers.

The passage goes on to state; *"But when they believed Philip as he preached good news about the kingdom of God and the name of Jesus Christ, they were baptized, both men and women. Even Simon himself believed, and after being baptized he continued with Philip. And seeing signs and great miracles performed, he was amazed"* (Acts 8:12-13).

It's obvious that after Simon came to faith, he lost his celebrity status among the locals. He was no longer perceived great, since he himself was being amazed by the miracles God performed through Philip. Simon now found himself operating on the periphery of the limelight, with Philip now the centre of attention. News of the success of Philip's ministry reached the Apostles in Jerusalem, who sent Peter and John to Samaria. Their mission was to pray with the new believers to receive the Holy Spirit through the laying on of their hands. As Peter and John prayed and laid their hands on the new believers, something remarkable happened.

Acts 8:17-23 states; *"Then they [Peter and John] laid their hands on them and they received the Holy Spirit.* **Now when Simon** [the former magician] **saw that the Spirit was given through the laying on of the apostles' hands, he offered them money, saying, "Give me this power also, so that anyone on whom I lay my hands may receive the Holy Spirit."** *But Peter said to him, "May your silver perish with you, because you thought you could obtain the gift of God with money! You have neither part nor lot in this matter, for your heart is not right before God. Repent, therefore, of this wickedness of yours, and pray to the Lord that, if possible, the intent of your heart may be forgiven you. For I see that you are in the gall of bitterness and in the bond of iniquity."*

Firstly, the passage is very clear that the power of the Holy Spirit is never for sale. The gift of healing, prayer, prophecy etc. are all not for sale in the body of Christ. These are free gifts the Holy Spirit manifests in the life of believers as He wills. The thought of freely giving such a precious gift (the Holy Spirit) must have been a shock to Simon, who was probably used to receiving payment for using his magic tricks. This man did not only receive the shock of his life, but also received a stern rebuke from Peter declining his lucrative gesture!

Aside the truth that the Holy Spirit is not for sale, why else would Peter decline such an offer? This was mainly due to Simon's motives, his level of spiritual maturity and the condition of his heart. Simon's motive was guided by his lust for power, money and fame. If Peter received payments for the gift of the Holy Spirit, he could in turn also receive payments for sharing this power with others. In his immature Christian view of life, this prospect was very lucrative. Furthermore, since the arrival of Philip, Simon had lost all his fame and recognition among the locals. Being a man of pride and arrogance, he desperately needed the power of the Holy Spirit to help reclaim his lost status. Simon could picture himself laying his hand on the highest bidder to receive the Holy Spirit. He could see this as the opportunity to get back into the limelight again.

Even though Simon had been baptised and had repented of his sins, including the practice of magic, he was still an immature Christian who was struggling with the issue of covetousness, attention-seeking and self-importance. Although he yearned for the power of the Holy Spirit and was even willing to pay for it, he did not receive it because his heart and motives were not right. Ultimately, Simon was an immature Christian who loved the Lord, but had much to learn prior to being entrusted with the precious gifts of the Holy Spirit.

We find that in the modern church, many believers are not fully experiencing the nature of their true identity in Christ. This is because similar to the case of Simon, while they are children of God and believers in Christ, they may unfortunately still be spiritually immature in faith and in character. Spiritual maturity is an essential quality that enables us to effectively represent the Kingdom and the King. It also helps us to use our authority and position for good and not for destructive self-seeking things. Spiritual maturity helps us to see and understand the nature of God more clearly, thereby rightfully living and teaching others His ways. Equally, it stands as a guard against heresy and false prophets. What the modern church really needs is spiritually mature believers who understand their identity in Christ, and are living this out as children of God and representative of the Kingdom.

Maturing In Your New Identity

MATURITY IN YOUR NEW IDENTITY

Life begins at conception in a mother's womb, and right from that moment growth is inevitable. One can never remain a baby forever so long as they have the breath of life in them. Life demands that we grow physically, mentally and emotionally, but never remaining the same. If physical growth is certain, so should our spiritual growth once we are born again and adopted into the Kingdom of God. Our physical growth is effectively sustained by the nourishment of various foods we eat on a daily basis. The variety of foods help in developing our physical wellbeing, considering that the various nutrients and vitamins contribute to specific functions that holistically makes us healthy people.

Similarly, our spiritual growth is effectively sustained by various factors. If one cannot expect full nourishment and development by eating the same food (e.g. plain boiled rice) daily, then a believer cannot expect to have attained full maturity by only believing in Jesus Christ as their Saviour. This does not imply that this believer is not saved, but rather that while he/she may have salvation, they may lack the full maturity after only taking the first few steps of faith and remaining content by that.

In John 15:5, the Lord said:

"I am the vine; you are the branches. Whoever abides in me and I in him, he it is that bears much fruit, for apart from me you can do nothing".

This passage encourages believers to have faith in the Lord Jesus Christ and abide in Him in order to bear much fruit. Before a branch bears fruit, it must have first reached the stage of maturity by abiding in the vine. Without maturity, there is no fruit; but most importantly, without abiding in the vine, there is no maturity. What does it mean to abide in Christ (the vine) then?

Abiding in Christ for maturity is essentially about fixing your eyes on Him and crowning Him king over every area of your life. It's about knowing Christ and being transformed more into His nature and likeness. Apostle Paul puts it beautifully by saying that the work of the ministers is to equip the saints *"until we all attain to the unity of the faith and of the knowledge of the Son of God,* **to mature manhood, to the measure of the stature of the fullness of Christ,***"* (Ephesians 4:13). Christ Jesus is therefore our standard of full maturity as children of God. But what can we do to further our maturity in Christ? Below detail some obvious examples we may sometimes overlook.

- Being a part of a church
- Reading and studying the Word of God
- Listening to sermons and reading Christian books
- Obeying and practicing biblical principles and teachings

Being a part of a church

I sometimes hear some Christians say that they prefer to do their own church at home, often meaning they don't want to fellowship with other believers in the traditional church setting. This idea is shaped by a few factors such as.

1) The modern individualistic view of society
2) A supposed new enlightenment they have found
3) Hurt by church members or find trends in church practices or culture unsettling.

While the third point has a valid reason for someone to consider this direction, it is still an unbiblical approach or option for a Christian to take.

Being part of a church brings you into fellowship with other believers where long-term friendships and relationships can be developed. In the modern western world where loneliness is such a big issue, the church can be the place that provides friendship and care for believers. In the church, you can also find community and various activities that can bring people together. Above all, in the church environment there is discipleship and leadership (shepherds) to nurture believers and ensure that the church is on the right path.

In my experience, I can say that most of the best teachings that shaped my life along the journey of faith has been in the church. My experience of encountering the power of the Holy Spirit with the gift of prophecy etc. was in the church. The opportunity to learn, serve and grow along the way was all because of the church. The church is called the Body of Christ for a reason. It is symbolic of each individual functioning as a limb. A limb that is detached from the body cannot grow or function on its own. Equally, if you desire maturity, being a part of a local church and actively engaging with believers is the first place to start.

Reading and studying the Word of God

The Bible is the Word of God that embodies the knowledge of His nature and an everlasting truth, spanning many generations and thousands of years. The Bible provides some historical information, giving us some insight into the nature of God's mercy, love, judgement, faithfulness etc. It also details various fulfilled prophecies and prophecies that are yet to be fulfilled. The Bible also has within it wonderful testimonies of men and women who have walked the path of faith with God, providing us with some examples and teachings we can learn and apply to our lives.

On reflecting on the importance of scripture and the integral part it plays in our lives, Paul said;

"For whatever was written in former days was written for our instruction, that through endurance and through the encouragement of the Scriptures we might have hope" (Romans 15:4).

The word of God therefore contains God's instructions to mankind, along with testimonies of how various men and women have lived in adherence to God's word or in disobedience to it. The consequences of their actions are also detailed to inform the present and future generation of the manner of life that pleases God, providing a form of guidance and counselling in decision making for maturity and hope.

As a child grows, they are dependent on the teachings of their parent's experiences, their school teacher's academic knowledge and the personal lessons they quickly learn from society through choices (good and bad) made by themselves and others. The Bible provides such diverse examples with lessons learnt, offering wisdom and advice that are knitted together by theological teachings and prophecies to holistically form a firm foundation of information upon which a believer can spiritually mature in their faith in Christ.

Without reading the Bible or indeed studying it, how would a new believer mature in their knowledge and understanding of the faith? Knowledge is based on the information you have concerning a subject area. The more knowledge you acquire, the greater your understanding of that subject.

A core theme of the Bible is **relationship**, most importantly, relationship between God and man, and relationship amongst mankind. The knowledge of understanding such relationship provides maturity in knowing the nature of God's love, mercy, kindness, faithfulness, grace among others, as well as knowing His laws, judgement and wrath.

Above all, understanding the transition of God's relationship with mankind from the old covenant to the new covenant provides the believer a good knowledge of their identity in Christ. The lack of such knowledge has led many captive to heretic teachings by those who confidently assert their misconception of God's truth.

In relation to this, the Lord spoke as detailed by Hosea the prophet, stating, *"My people are destroyed for lack of knowledge; because you have rejected knowledge, I reject you from being a priest to me. And since you have forgotten the law of your God, I also will forget your children"* (Hosea 4:6).

This message was written to the priests of the house of Israel, of whom the Lord had appointed to teach the knowledge of His word to His people. God lamented through Hosea the prophet on how evil had abounded in the land as a direct result of the lack of knowledge the priests had with regards to His laws and commandments. The issue here was not because they did not teach the people, but rather, they taught the people the wrong things, since they themselves lacked in the knowledge of truth.

One may draw the conclusion that this passage relates only to the priests and shepherds placed in charge of the ministry, but the truth is, one of our identities in Christ Jesus is that we are all **royal priesthoods** (1 Peter 2:9). This implies that, while we have pastors and teachers to provide a better and deeper knowledge of God's Word, the believer also shares in the responsibility of studying the word and maturing in understanding the knowledge of truth for them self.

In writing to Timothy, Paul the Apostle of Christ exhorted him by saying,

"Study to shew thyself approved unto God, a workman that needeth not to be ashamed, rightly dividing the word of truth" (2 Timothy 2:15) KJV.

Apostle Paul said this to Timothy, not because he was not versed in the theological teachings of the Gospel of faith, but rather because Paul understood the great responsibility placed on the shoulders of church leaders (according to their various gifts and offices) to effectively labour in ensuring the maturity of the church in Christ. The knowledge and spiritual maturity of church leaders may reflect the maturity of the church. For this reason, Paul also said;

"And he (Christ Jesus) gave the apostles, the prophets, the evangelists, the shepherds and teachers, to equip the saints for the work of ministry, for building up the body of Christ, until we all attain to the unity of the faith and of the knowledge of the Son of God, to mature manhood, to the measure of the stature of the fullness of Christ, so that we may no longer be children, tossed to and fro by the waves and carried about by every wind of doctrine, by human cunning, by craftiness in deceitful schemes" (Ephesians 4:11-14).

It is a shame that in the current body of Christ, some "pastors" have undermined the importance of understanding and maturing in God's Word, and have opted for the fast-track of being teachers without much knowledge of the truth. Some have done so out of a genuine passion for the great commission of Christ, while others have embarked on this to further their deceptive schemes for personal gain. Subsequently, what you will have is spiritual babies leading other babies, with some teaching heresies that have no part in the Gospel of Christ. Ultimately, it is the believers that are affected, but more so, the believers that do not study the Word for themselves.

In personal studying, there are always new revelations by the Holy Spirit, a reminder of the Word of truth, a comparative reflection of God's Word on oneself, and maturity in faith through the knowledge of truth. By maturing in the knowledge of God's word, one becomes more aware of their identity in Christ, making them secured and firmly established in their faith and being able to rightly discern between the word of truth and deceptive religious (and worldly) teachings.

Listening to sermons and reading other Christian books

Listening to sermons

Sermons and teachings are essential in furthering a believer's maturity in Christ. The spoken Word of God in the form of a preach is so powerful it changes the course of many lives. Our words carry power and life in it. We are essentially shaped by our experiences in life and the many words spoken to us; so, do not underestimate the power of words. Some people have a confidence about them and a positive outlook in life. Others lack self-confidence and may face life with despair or uncertainty. While many factors and experiences may account for this, the power of words spoken to them plays a key part in shaping their outlook in life.

A few years ago, I served as one of the youth workers in a local church in Croydon. Working with the young people, I noticed that generally the youth were very confident about everything, even things they didn't know much about. They were a very energetic bunch who were willing to give anything a try. Often, they are over confident of their ability when in reality their confidence does not actually match their ability. What I noticed was that they weren't afraid to fail and keep trying, but what actually fuelled this motivation was words of encouragement spoken by leaders. Words like, "you can do it", "that was brilliant", "that was close" etc. goes a long way in empowering them and making them better.

Equally, the spoken Word of God in a preach or a sermon carries life in it. It has the power to shape us and mould us more into the likeness of Christ. A good sermon has some vital nutrients within it to help the spiritual man grow in faith. So important is the spoken word of God that Jesus said, if it falls on fertile grounds i.e. when it is heard and received by the believer, it produces fruits yielding a hundred folds, sixty folds etc. (Matthew 13:23). But in the same way, so important is the spoken Word of God that Jesus said, *"When anyone hears the word of the kingdom and does not understand it, the evil one comes and snatches away what has been sown in his heart"* (Matthew 13:19). The Word of God is so important that the devil himself will try and prevent you from hearing it. No wonder we see some believers sleeping during sermons on a Sunday. Sometimes you can't blame them because some speakers can be very boring; but essentially, it highlights ways that the devil tries to snatch the spoken Word of God needed for our maturity.

Along my journey of faith, I have found listening to sermons very helpful in developing my understanding and enabling spiritual growth. I would however advice that it should be perceived as an essential supplement or starters to the meal, rather than the whole meal itself. What I mean is, our hope for spiritual maturity should not only rest on listening to weekly sermons, but also in digging deeper in our study of the Word and general reading of other Christian books.

Reading other Christian books

The Bible is the complete and sufficient Word of God from which all believers are encouraged to eat and drink for their spiritual maturity. The Bible is also a source of inspiration for many Christian authors who have been uniquely impacted by this Word of truth through their personal journey with the Lord.

The Bible will forever remain constant, having the same teachings from Genesis to Revelation. On the other hand, the testimonies and knowledge of other believers may provide us with some fresh insights into understanding the nature of God and His work in this day and age.

Our unique identity as individuals provides variations in ability, talents, knowledge and expertise. For this reason, God has given to the body of Christ, men and women with a passion and the capability to methodically research the word of God and provide details in an expatiating manner that can aid other believers to clearly understand the Bible. Some of these men and women have written books as led by the Holy Spirit to share their knowledge of the Word of God through academic and other written materials. These individuals may have their personal reasons for writing, but the ultimate essence of this is for the body of Christ to attain maturity by such knowledge.

Other Christian authors have been through various experiences in their journey with the Lord, and have been encouraged to share their testimonies with the world. Testimonies are to encourage the body of Christ, giving personal details of non-biblical individuals of whom we can all relate to. Often, many believers have viewed biblical individuals as somewhat 'superhuman', hence they have found it challenging to relate to their experiences. God has given to the church, believers like you and I, who have been through various experiences and have found the Lord to be faithful and true in their personal encounters. Some of the testimonies may be about God's salvation, healing, provision, direction, rebuke etc. while others may be about supernatural experiences of heaven, hell or interactions with angels and demons. All of these experiences and personal testimonies provide the body of Christ with wealth of information concerning the nature of God, the spiritual world and the diverse relationship God has with believers from past to present generations even after the Bible had been written. Some of these testimonies are ultimately written as directed by the Holy Spirit to equip the body of Christ with the knowledge and experiences of others, leading to maturity and a better understanding of who God is.

Advances in technology has also paved ways for believers to easily access information through search engines and social media sites, where information is made available at the click of a button. The variety of choices in the format of data (i.e videos, audio and written data), grants every willing believer their preferred choice of accessing information. What will the excuse of this generation be for not knowing God more intimately and maturing in the faith? I am not exempted from this question, as I wonder what my excuse will be.

While we have all of this wealth of information that can be easily accessible, believers may however need to be more discerning with regards to the books they read, videos they watch and audios they listen to, considering the Bible have often warned of false prophets and teachers who can be equally zealous in their heretic and deceptive teachings (Matthew 7:15).

A famous underlining quote to advice believers to exercise discernment in what they read (or in modern day, what they watch or listen to), says, *"Visit many good books, but live in the Bible."* (Charles H Spurgeon).

Obeying and practicing biblical principles and teachings

The nurturing of every child from birth to a stage of independence is often through verbal communication and other means that guides and teaches the child of the way of life. The natural tendencies of most children are to obey their parents, though some disobey out of innocence and ignorance of the consequences of their actions. In the years of a child's development, many instructions (do's and don'ts) and advice are given to a child, and it is their level of obedience (application, practice, following, living out etc.) to these instructions that could determine their safety, wellbeing and subsequent avoidance of undesirable outcomes. The book of proverbs has much advice with regards to this, some of a few are as follows:

Proverbs 13:1 *"A wise son hears his father's instruction, but a scoffer does not listen to rebuke"*.

The notion of hearing as stated in this proverb has a literal meaning of one who follows instructions, since it is the act of obedience to that instruction that makes the advice beneficial to the child.

Proverbs 15:32 *"Whoever ignores instruction despises himself, but he who listens to reproof gains intelligence"*.

Good instruction and advice is always for one's own benefit, despising them could equally mean ignoring warning signs and blatant danger that can impede on one's safety and wellbeing.

Proverbs 15:10 *"There is severe discipline for him who forsakes the way; whoever hates reproof will die"*.

This proverb points to the extreme consequences of one who despises instructions, advice and reproof. The proverb indicates that disobedience can lead to severe consequences and hard lessons learnt, while in extreme cases may result to death.

These few proverbs highlight a significant life principle, indicating that obedience always has its benefits and disobedience, its consequences. The ability to heed and obey instructions plays a vital role in a child's development and subsequent maturity in engaging with the world around him or her. The alternative could be as a result of disobedience, ignorance and general life experiences from which a person could carefully learn lessons from. The process of learning from experience (most often from past successes and mistakes) helps to develop one's understanding of life's principles, leading to maturity and enabling them to effectively make the right decisions, judgements and choices in similar future circumstances.

Similarly, as believers in Christ, our obedience and adherence to godly teachings are beneficial to our spiritual wellbeing and maturity in faith. But our disobedience to these principles may lead to consequences, of which our understanding of its extent may vary.

The writer of the book of James exhorts believers to be doers of the word and not hearers only. In James 1:22-25, the writer states; *"But be doers of the word, and not hearers only, deceiving yourselves. For if anyone is a hearer of the word and not a doer, he is like a man who looks intently at his natural face in a mirror. For he looks at himself and goes away and at once forgets what he was like. But the one who looks into the perfect law, the law of liberty, and perseveres, being no hearer who forgets but a doer who acts, he will be blessed in his doing"*.

Apostle Paul reiterates this point in Romans 2:13, as he said; *"For it is not the hearers of the law who are righteous before God, but the doers of the law who will be justified"*.

[**Note**: *The context in which Apostle Paul made this statement in Romans 2:13; does not imply that believers are justified by keeping of the law, since we (Christians) are justified by grace through faith in Christ Jesus.*]

It is important to understand that obedience and applying one's effort and will to live a righteous life isn't legalism. Some believers have somehow come to the conclusion that once they are born again and found in Christ, they shouldn't even try or make an effort to do something that will demand too much of their will to live righteously. If you appear to show any sense of striving for righteousness or intentionally wanting to live a godly life, some may label you as a legalist. While we all know that Christ is our righteousness and we cannot add to His finished work, it is important to note that spiritual maturity also demands a change in character and lifestyle.

Earthly maturity is often visible by a change in the conduct of a person, from childhood behaviour to a morally acceptable standard expected of adults. Maturity in the faith can also be noticeable by a believer's genuine application of biblical teachings and principles as led by the Holy Spirit, and as seen in a change in their moral conduct. To this end, Apostle Paul urged the church of Colossae and Laodicea to 'put off' or 'put to death' the sinful practices that identified them with their old unregenerate self; and to 'put on' the character and nature of Christ, which was now their new identity (Colossians 3:5-17).

Ultimately, a 'believer' who is relaxed about following biblical teachings with regards to morality, will eventually not only face the natural consequences, but will undoubtedly portray or misrepresent the nature and character of the Kingdom.

Example: A few of the attribute of Christ Jesus is honesty and faithfulness, since He is the exact imprint of God the Father (Hebrews 1:3). A believer who knows of this but yet is caught in an act of theft or fraud, will not only suffer the consequences and disgrace, but will have misrepresented the nature of God to others. It is therefore the obedience and practice of biblical principles that provides the world with evidence that we a new in Christ Jesus. The old identity with its corrupt practices has passed away and the new identity with the Christ-like nature is evident. This is the character of God in the Gospel we preach, to which those in darkness see and are drawn to the light.

Similar to the development of our individual habits, the Christ-like nature and its habits become a part of one's lifestyle. Through our obedience to the Holy Spirit and application of biblical teachings, we can then live a Christ-like life that leads us further into maturity.

Finally, a word of encouragement.

You are a Child of God now, a Kingdom Citizen, a Royal Priesthood, an Ambassador for Christ, one in whom the Spirit of God dwells. Be bold and courageous and let your light shine as a testimony of the Gospel on to others. Let the world know what country (Heaven) man or woman you really are. Be blessed by this knowledge of your identity in Christ Jesus, and reach out to those in darkness with the light the dwells in you.

May the God who has adopted you and crowned you with such glory, lead you and guide you all the days of your life. May He reveal Himself to you in a greater measure as you journey through life with Christ. Hope to see you in the new Heaven and the new Earth one day.

Blessings,

Chris Eke